A HOMELAND DENIED

IN THE FOOTSTEPS OF A POLISH POW

IRENA KOSSAKOWSKI

Whittles Publishing

Published by
Whittles Publishing Ltd.,
Dunbeath,
Caithness, KW6 6EG,
Scotland, UK

www.whittlespublishing.com

© 2016 Irena Kossakowski
reprinted 2017

ISBN 978-184995-264-4

Printed by Charlesworth Press, Wakefield

CONTENTS

ACKNOWLEDGEMENTS

Thanks are due to the many people who gave their time to help with this book:

Agnetha Olicki, Kris Rezlar, Izabelle Iperro, Rita Fairchild, Carole and John Gunstone, Rachel and Bryan Roberts, Peter Rixon, Margaret Harvey, Patsy Dunton, Ann Rossiter, Hayley and Chris Rutherford, Chris Derrick, Darren Clarke, Andrzej Kossakowski, and Lynn Clarke nee Kossakowski, with special thanks to Pauline Cole.

I also record my thanks to:

Tim Bucknall, Anna Pacewicz, Kresy-Siberia.org

Dr. Andrzej Suchcitz, Archives, Polish Institute and Sikorski Museum, London

Judith Coote, Monte Cassino Society

Bata Reminiscence and Resource Centre, East Tilbury, Essex

Pat Arehart, Harbour Bookshop, Kingsbridge

Michael Chequer, BBC Radio Devon

Michal Kubicki, Polish Radio

and Feliks Konarski, for *Red Poppies of Monte Cassino/Czerwone maki na Monte Cassino*

IN MEMORY OF MY FATHER,
WACLAW PIOTR KOSSAKOWSKI

and dedicated to his best friend and my Godfather, Basyl Lesowiec,
and all the many unrecognised Poles who fought for your freedom and ours

PREFACE

When I was young, I wasn't really that interested in what had happened during the war. That's understandable for a young person for whom even 20 years seems ages ago.

I knew my Dad had nightmares of course. It was something we had grown up with and never paid much heed to. After Dad had left for work much earlier, we would mention it at the breakfast table. His shouting had kept us awake again, what was he shouting about? But of course, being in Polish, Mum couldn't understand what he was saying and would only say it was to do with the war.

I cringe now at how unfeeling I was then. His birthday was on 19 May, just a day after the Poles had raised the flag at Monte Cassino, but he never spoke about it, not a word, until so many years later. I knew he came from another country of course. Being the only 'foreigner' at school with a name that no one could ever pronounce made sure of that and naturally our accent meant we sounded different. Dad's accent was very strong then and changed little over the years. He could never say the word 'the', only 'za' and similarly 'zat', 'zem' and 'zere.' Even now when I talk fast I lapse into this style!

I was ten when he first returned to Poland. Mum was panic-stricken he would not be coming back and worried he could be imprisoned. That was inconceivable to me. I thought people went to prison for stealing things, not merely visiting another country. Why would he go to prison? But he did, for a week, and they took most of his money and all his gifts. But he did come home and as the international situation became easier he returned every year, even taking my Mum with him years later.

Poland wasn't a country anyone really knew about. It wasn't mentioned much at school other than being on the map and a communist country. Dad never spoke too much about it, though he did paint the house bricks red and white, the colours of the Polish flag, much to Mum's annoyance!

Watching movies like 'The Great Escape' I commented on what a nice place it was for a prison camp – they got chocolate, food parcels and hot showers. That was when Dad got up and switched off the T.V. 'Chocolate,' he shouted, 'hot water!' He was angry but also very upset although I didn't really understand why and when I asked later, he just said the Russians didn't believe in the Geneva Convention, there was no Red Cross or food parcels and he had to wash in the snow. That was my first real inkling that life during the war must have been very different to the movies...for some anyway.

Many years later, my youngest son Darren had to write a small piece about his Grandad. Dad drew a map and wrote a small piece about his life in the camp and the army. When asked about it later, Darren replied that it hadn't been chosen to be read aloud, as it wasn't interesting enough. I remember seeing the sadness in Dad's eyes and only then did I begin to understand how much he had gone through and what he had suffered. To write even just a brief account brought the memories flooding back, they never really left him. To be told it wasn't interesting enough must have hurt. I knew then that I had to find out more – to create a record for my children and grandchildren, so they would know about his life, because it deserved to be remembered.

Very little was known due to the strict Russian censorship. The Poles were not allowed to attend the Victory Parade in Britain – at the insistence of the Russian leader. In Poland, nothing could be published or even talked about. Atrocities like the Katyn massacre were denied and even blamed on others. As my Dad remarked sadly when hearing President Gorbachev eventually admit responsibility, all they had to do was ask a Pole. All the movies and books were about the Germans, the Holocaust and the Russians; and rightly so of course, nothing should ever be forgotten. But what little mention there was of Poland, the bravery and the heroism, was glossed over or even attributed to other countries.

So little by little I chipped away at Dad, trying to get him to open up and the more I discovered, the more deeply saddened I became that this had happened to my father and others like him. At last I understood the nightmares.

I hope you find this story enlightening, interesting and ultimately uplifting – at least now the true story has been told.

Irena Kossakowski

FOREWORD

MEMORY HAS NOT LET HERSELF BE DESTROYED, DID NOT SUCCUMB TO VIOLENCE

QUOTE FROM THE POEM 'KATYN' BY FELIKS KONARSKI (PSEUDONYM 'REF-REN')

Although Waclaw Kossakowski was spared the fate of his fellow prisoners in Kozielsk and the unexpected horrors of Katyn Forest, his journey was still full of terrible experiences in an 'inhuman land'. As a forced labourer in one of the most inhospitable places in the world he became part of the tragic Polish history under Stalin's regime and Soviet brutality.

Irena Kossakowski undertook the challenging journey of recording her father's story to encourage new generations to understand Polish history during World War II and how the Polish people had been denied their homeland for so many years.

Meeting Irena in Katyn Museum was an amazing experience and truly the completion of much hard work to once again unite Polish survivors of Soviet dictatorship from all over the world. If only more descendants of Polish refugees would be as engaged as Irena.

Paweł Warczyński
Katyn Museum

ONE

RUSSIA, NEAR THE WHITE SEA, NOVEMBER 1939

THE SOUL OF POLAND IS INDESTRUCTIBLE, AND SHE WILL RISE AGAIN LIKE A ROCK WHICH MAY FOR A SPELL BE SUBMERGED BY A TIDAL WAVE, BUT WHICH REMAINS A ROCK.

WINSTON CHURCHILL, 1 OCTOBER 1939

The wooden cattle trucks rattled laboriously along at an uneven pace, their cold metal wheels clattering noisily on the iron railway tracks, jolting their occupants.

The bitter Arctic wind easily found its way through the poorly fitted slats of wood, chilling the fifty men inside each truck. Crammed like sardines shoulder to shoulder, they were unable even to move their arms from their sides, and the suffocating smell of unwashed bodies combined with the overpowering stench of urine and vomit was nauseating.

Pressed tightly into a far corner of the truck was a young Polish soldier, fresh from Warsaw University. Without any warning, Germany had invaded Poland on 1 September 1939, and Vadek Kossakowski had volunteered immediately on hearing the news. But the Poles were hopelessly outnumbered as the Germans advanced with over one million troops on several fronts – and when Soviet forces unexpectedly invaded from the east just two weeks later, Warsaw had to admit defeat. However, the Polish government never officially surrendered, and its exiled leaders fled to London while its people continued to fight with the Underground, the Polish resistance movement.

Under a Soviet agreement with Hitler which remained in force until June 1941 – and which had included a secret protocol to partition conquered territories – Poland was now split between Germany and Russia. The Soviets took the eastern half, and almost two million Polish citizens were sent to labour camps in Siberia. Here they would be forced to build runways in readiness for the military airbases Stalin planned to construct there.

Vadek remembered only too well the brutality of the Russian prison on the outskirts of Kozielsk village, one hundred and fifty miles from the capital of Moscow and ninety from the city of Smolensk. With the other cadets from the army training school who had been arrested that grim day of 19 September, he had endured several months of interrogation and harsh treatment in the detention centre on the Polish border with Latvia, before being taken to Kozielsk (in Russia).

Once the centre had been the important Orthodox monastery Optina Pustyn, comprising a chapel and several outbuildings connected by long corridors centred around a large and tranquil quadrangle – but now it served as a military prison. With views across the pine forests and gentle rolling hills not far from the river, its peaceful, rather quaint, setting belied its now forbidding interior.

He had been desperately scared, wondering if he could endure another beating, unable to prevent himself from shaking whenever he heard those heavy boots echoing on the hard stone floor as they came slowly and menacingly nearer to his bare but filthy cell. At each dreaded footfall along that long narrow corridor, he had frozen, as if moving would in some way bring that which he feared closer toward him. Hardly even daring to breathe, he felt that every fibre of his being was stretched taut with fearful trepidation as they reached his door; almost collapsing with relief when they passed. If they passed; sometimes they did not.

Every day there were incessant interrogations, and roll calls at all hours of the day and night. His name, his identity, was taken from him, and from that day forth he answered to a cold, impersonal number.

He wasn't brave, or did not think so. No-one he knew of had been prepared for war, and events had escalated so quickly there was no option but to fight. Kill or be killed. There was no other choice – but the only thing he had had brandished before was a pen, for he was a mathematician not a soldier. Though not particularly religious, but brought up in the Catholic faith as most Poles were, he now found himself uttering a prayer more frequently than he had ever done before. Death was always at the forefront of his mind, and he did not want to die. The terrible uncertainty consumed him every day, and he felt he was trapped in a terrifying nightmare with no possibility of waking up.

And his family, what of them? He had so desperately wanted to get a message to them, but there had been no warning of the approaching Red Army. And no time. No time to do anything, for it had all happened so quickly. How could he have sent it anyhow – who would have taken it? There was no-one. Now it was too late. No-one knew where he was or where he was going.

But he did. He was on his way to Siberia. He had not known what to expect and had been terrified that he would be shot like so many others. Every day he had been asked to give up his Polish citizenship, to deny his heritage. But he had not. He would not.

Then one cold grey dawn he had heard his number called, followed by a loud hammering on the door before it was pushed open and a surly guard brusquely ordered him out of his cell. With the other men milling around in the corridors, he had assembled in the central compound where, stamping their feet against the bitter cold, the men were kept waiting for several long minutes. Wondering what was going to happen, they debated quietly amongst themselves, only falling silent when a Russian official strode into the courtyard and informed them, in cold, clipped tones, they were being moved to another camp. A better place, they were told, where they could work for the good of the Soviet Union.

There were some murmurings among the former cadets, but the general concept was that it must, surely, be a better place. But Vadek had been unsure, and was wary of anything the Russians said, for there had been so many different rumours circulating; it was difficult to know what to believe. They all so badly wanted to believe in something good; desperation deprived them of rational thinking.

And he was right to be distrustful, for it was not to be, and reports slowly filtered through that they were being transported to the worst possible place a man could have gone to. The cruel wasteland that was Siberia.

It was the most appalling news, but at least Vadek was still alive. For now.

Each man was searched, and items such as penknives, pens, writing paper, scissors were all confiscated. When the guard found the photograph of his family, Vadek started in dismay, forcing himself not to reach out and retrieve it or look concerned. But after studying it for several seconds, the guard returned it to him, with his blanket – a coarse horsehair blanket that his mother had woven for him – and, laughing derisively, said that Vadek would need it where he was going.

Outside, the early morning air was damp and chilly. The prisoners were herded to waiting lorries for the trip to Kozielsk railway station, some five miles distant. Here they were marched to the sidings and herded into the trucks.

With the exception of the photograph and his blanket, Vadek had nothing. Nothing at all other than the clothes he wore. He was not alone. It was all any man had.

Siberia … surely there wasn't any more inhospitable place on earth. A white wilderness where even in the summer the ground remained frozen and the biting winds never ceased to blow. A truly unforgiving place. If there was such a place as hell, then this was surely it. And there could be no escape from a Siberian gulag.

In the truck, he pressed his face against the wood and gulped the air blowing in through a slit, gasping as it hit his lungs. Being pinned against an outer wall was colder than in the middle; however, with less chance of suffocation from lack of air and the sheer weight of bodies squeezing the last breath from his own, he had a slightly higher chance of survival. In the centre, a hole in the floor was intended as a latrine, but it was impossible for nearly everyone to use it, as they were unable to move.

Peering through one of the slits, Vadek watched the landscape roll by, broken only by clumps of tall, straggly pines, their branches stretched towards the sky and the watery grey sun, as if they too were crying out for warmth. Never changing, nothing to shock, excite or entertain the eye. Just endless miles of hostile, desolate wilderness.

His eye caught some markings on the wood near to him. Peering more closely, he realised with a shock they were a date and a name scratched into the wood, presumably with a nail. As he scrutinised the walls next to him, he noticed there were more. Some in black slate, others scratched in anything that had come to hand. He realised with dismay that there had been other men in this same truck, men on the same awful journey and trying to leave a sign, a record of their being there, to show others who might come after them that they shared the same fate. Whatever that was.

It was a harrowing thought that pierced Vadek to the very core of his being with its sombre finality. Able only to move his head, his mouth so dry it was difficult to form any words, he turned it to face the man next to him. But words were not necessary. The cadet next to him was dead. Eyes glassy, unseeing, body held upright by the men next to him. Vadek closed his eyes in disbelief and shock. How many more? he thought, and how long before he too would succumb? Surely it was only a matter of time.

Twice a day the train would stop, and the prisoners could relieve themselves while the guards rapidly and dispassionately cleared the trucks of the dead and dying. For if a man was unable to stand, he was unable to work and of no use to the Russians. Corpses thrown from previous trains lined the route, partly covered with fallen snow. It was a sight Vadek would never be able to erase from his memory, and it came back to haunt him throughout the years, long after the war had ended.

And there were many stops when the transportees were not allowed out at all. Then came the sound of the guards' feverish activity as they jumped down from the train, followed by the metallic clangs of shovels as they scraped the mechanism free of ice. The door would be opened just long enough for a bucket of water to be passed in, and chunks of hard bread quickly pushed into grasping, outstretched hands before it was slammed shut again. The occasional salted herring was thrown in too, but the men soon realised that it was better to leave those, for no water was given afterwards and the salt made their lips dry, cracking and bleeding.

With a sigh Vadek closed his eyes and thought longingly of home, wondering if he would ever see his family again. Did they even know he was alive? Upon leaving the university he had immediately reported to a cadet military training camp, but with just two weeks of training at the time of the invasion, they had been ill equipped both physically and mentally, and had quickly been taken prisoner by the invading Red Army.

What was he doing here anyway? He had never wanted to be a soldier; he was going to be a teacher. Andrzei was the soldier. Vadek wondered what had happened to his cousin, and a smile flickered across his worn features as memories of happier times filled his tired mind.

He could see his mother, busily baking in the kitchen of the small timber farmhouse. And there was his little brother Roman with his fingers in the dough for her home-made *pączki*, Polish-style jam-filled doughnuts, shoving as much as he could into his mouth before his mother caught him.

Vadek's pinched face softened as his mind drifted, and, as he nodded off, in the foggy realms of half-sleep he could hear his mother calling …

He was jolted back to reality as the train shuddered to a halt, the icy wheels screeching against the icy track. He stumbled and would have fallen had there been enough room to fall. Outside he could hear shouts in Russian. Dogs were barking aggressively and the crunching of footsteps on frozen ground came ominously nearer.

Brilliant white daylight flooded into the truck as the door was wrenched noisily open on its stiff metal runners. The men inside blinked and tried to shield their eyes from the glare, momentarily blinded after hours of gloom in the windowless trucks. Dazed, they staggered out as if drunk, their limbs stiff from inactivity and cold.

The below zero temperature hit them like a whack with an icy wet towel. Jumping up and down, they furiously flapped their arms about their bodies and against their sides, batting their hands together and blowing through frozen fingers in an attempt to keep warm. After enduring almost twenty-one long, harrowing days they had arrived at Murmansk. It was far north of the Arctic Circle, but due to the warming influence of the Gulf Stream, its waters were ice-free all year round. Here they would board boats taking them to their final destination in the desolate outer reaches of the Kola peninsula.

The guards moved quickly along the side of the train, shoving the living men away from the trucks as they impassively dragged out the dead from inside, throwing them carelessly to the side of the tracks to land in the snow, as if they were nothing more than sacks of mouldy potatoes.

Sickened and deeply saddened by the loss of his comrades and unable to comprehend the inhumanity of his guards, Vadek looked away and tried to concentrate on his surroundings.

Never had he seen such a vast expanse of nothingness. No fertile farmland here – only a few sparse clumps of straggly bushes poking out through the hard snow. A few lean fir trees, bleakly outlined against the stark backdrop of greyish sky and frozen wastes, gave the only clue that there was a horizon. The sheer harshness was in itself blinding, making the men screw up their haggard faces and squint.

But they were not allowed to stand still for long, as they were shoved onward with rifle butts. Guard dogs snapped and snarled at the prisoners' heels as they were propelled in single file towards the jetty. Boarding the boats, they huddled together in small groups. Fur hatflaps were pulled well down over the ears and the collars of their greatcoats turned up to reach the cheekbones in a vain effort to block the howling winds. Their icy breath resembled billowing smoke as it curled up into the freezing air.

No-one spoke. As the boats chugged out into the icy waters of the Barents Sea, they stood silently and watched with hollow eyes and gaunt faces, until they were herded below deck.

There, the conditions were almost as abysmal as in the cattle trucks, with well over a thousand men crammed onto each boat and with less than fifteen minutes a day allowed on deck. With no beds and no space even to sit down on the floor, the men slept where they stood. It was a breeding ground for sickness and disease, and dead prisoners were routinely thrown into the icy waters. These men had endured so much in the most inhumane of conditions on a journey of over three thousand miles, only for it to end here.

The voyage took three nightmarish days. Many became violently seasick and were too ill to muster the energy to venture on deck for the brief time they were allowed. However, the horrendous conditions and the oppressive atmosphere forced Vadek up on top whenever he had the opportunity. Growing up on a farm, he had always preferred to be outside and felt uneasy in confined spaces. As a consequence, he would often brave the outside temperatures and grip his blanket tightly over his shoulders as he paced the open deck.

The pale polar sun low on the horizon generated no perceivable heat, and the wind was unrelenting in its ferocity as the boats hugged the coastline, never venturing far into the open water for fear of mines lurking just beneath the surface.

Occasionally, a solitary seal broke the monotony of the landscape as it swam alongside or hitched a ride on one of the many ice floes. Always there was the continuous sound of the ice cracking, and this was occasionally heralded by long, eerie groans followed by a loud thunderous clap. Then a giant iceberg would break up and fall into the icy waters with a resounding crash that echoed far into the stillness. Here no birds sang; they were noticeable only by their absence. Vadek hadn't realised how much he missed their uplifting songs. Surely there could be no more desolate place on earth, for the Arctic was doomed by nature to be a perpetual frigidness that would never experience enough of the warmth of the sun's rays to blossom.

Late in the afternoon of the third day after leaving Murmansk, the boats docked at a small settlement. As the men stepped ashore, many had trouble finding their 'land legs', swaying about unsteadily as if still at sea. A faint smile crossed Vadek's features as he saw several of their guards with the same problem.

Tarpaulin-covered trucks were waiting for them to continue their journey, and for several hours they lurched over the uneven frozen ground. Vadek was seated next to one of the two guards that accompanied them, his rifle lying across his knees. The Russian's features barely flickered as he kept his eyes fixed straight ahead. Vadek wondered if he felt as cold and miserable as the rest of them. No one was allowed to talk even if they had wanted to, and the journey passed in silence.

It was almost impossible to guess how much time had elapsed before the trucks at the front of the convoy eventually stopped. Unable to see out, the men could only assume they had arrived, and they were not wrong. The tarpaulins were lifted, and the prisoners were curtly ordered to step down. Vadek was the last, jumping out shakily onto stiff, cold legs. He straightened and stretched his cramped muscles slowly, while looking about and assessing his surroundings.

This, then, was the prisoner of war camp. Camp Kola. A gulag built decades earlier on the orders of Stalin to house enemies of the state: Russians who had directly opposed the cruel rule of the Soviet leader, and unwary civilians who had dared to utter a word of complaint at the wrong time or in the wrong place.

The gulag was a truly daunting sight, and Vadek felt a strong gut reaction in response to his nervous apprehension. Filled with such a terrible sense of foreboding, the like of which he had never experienced before, he felt physically sick. It was surreal. He was twenty years old and he was afraid. Afraid of the unknown. Afraid of what the future might hold and afraid of dying in this godforsaken place. The gulag was something to be feared, for death was surely the only way out.

The double iron gates loomed in front of him, and with each quaking step he felt as if he were walking to his doom. For one brief second – so quick it was gone before he could properly grasp it – he was consumed by the desire to take flight, before those huge gates closed behind him and he was trapped like a bird in a cage. To run. Run now! Before the moment was lost … but as soon as the thought entered his head, it had gone. Replaced with the more rational one. Where? Where would he go?

So many chaotic thoughts flashed through his mind. To die … die slowly, frozen to death in the middle of this horrendous desolation. Or to cling on to life, however awful it might be … to survive … to endure and to hope … hope there would be a way out. Somehow. Please, God, don't let me die here …

Stilling his wild thoughts, Vadek flicked a glance up at the sentry towers. Two guards had their machine guns trained directly on him. Averting his gaze, he looked around him curiously.

Double barbed-wire fences over ten feet high ran along the perimeter of the camp, broken by twenty-foot sentry towers at each corner and at regular intervals along the wire. Housed in each tower was a Russian guard, his rifle at the ready and far too eager to shoot anyone who stepped out of line. At night, searchlights swept continuously through the camp, illuminating every corner. Sentries marching back and forth patrolled the boundaries, barely able to control their dogs. Teeth bared and ears laid flat against their heads, there was aggressiveness in their every movement as they barked at the newcomers.

The huge gates slowly swung open, grating on the icy ground. The men shuffled through them into the compound. As they passed through the gateway the guards counted them: five, five, five … The barbed-wire fencing of the inner enclosure faced them, while beyond the wire lay long barracks submerged in snow with dugout channels running beside each row. These led to other points in the camp, all surrounded by high barbed-wire fences. Set in blocks of six rows were several timber huts, and beyond these yet more barbed wire.

When the men had been counted and were assembled, the camp commandant strode into the area and onto a small podium. Raising a megaphone to his mouth he called sharply for attention and in an emotionless voice announced:

Rule No. 1 – You don't work, you don't eat.

Rule No. 2 – When marching in columns, keep to one step to the left and one to the right. Break formation and the guards will shoot to kill.

Rule No. 3 – Mind the death zones, 10 feet inside the barbed wire. There will be no mercy. Step into them and the guards will shoot to kill.

Rule No. 4 – There is to be no attempt to escape. Any prisoner caught will be shot. If the guards do not kill you, you will perish in the tundra. Look around you. There is nowhere to run to. This place will be your grave.

Stunned into silence, the men were split into groups of a hundred or so; each group was marched across the compound to one of the wooden huts, where they were roughly pushed inside. Bare floorboards creaked as Vadek moved wearily to one of the bunks in the centre and, hitching himself up onto the top one, he sat there, legs dangling, taking a moment to take stock of his surroundings as the other men filed into the room.

Each hut was filled with four rows of three-tier bunks. Their occupants had no belongings nor was there room for them; with barely a foot between each bed, conditions were terribly cramped. A single light bulb glared starkly from the middle of the ceiling.

Vadek lay back on the wooden board that was his bed. He was thankful for the blanket, and it had served him well in keeping out the winds and rain. Folding his hands behind his head for a pillow, he stared up at the ceiling and closed his eyes. Exhausted and hungry, he tried to think of anything but food.

His thoughts turned again to his cousin Andrzei, and he wondered where he was and what he was doing. He hoped he was in more hospitable surroundings, for anywhere would surely be better than where Vadek was now.

He remembered his comrades at the university in Warsaw and the last time they had been together. There had been no hesitation on hearing the news. Everyone had volunteered immediately, full of hope and valour, all eager to do what they could to protect their homeland. Six young men on the brink of war. Something none of them had envisaged and none of them had planned for. Ordinary men living ordinary lives; until now. What did fate have in store for any of them? For Poland?

The small cafe/bar situated just round the corner from the University of Warsaw had been a regular meeting place for students. Here he had come so often to meet with friends away from their studies at the end of the day. But the jollity and banter that day had been marred by the worry of an uncertain future, for they had heard of several skirmishes along the borders and no one could be sure of anything any more.

But there had been other, more cheerful things to talk about, and Vadek remembered fondly how his friends had teased him about a girl. He had laughed, protesting that they were just friends, nothing more. Where was Ana now, he wondered. Was she his girl? Maybe. If things had been different. Nothing had been said, no words spoken, just an understanding …

He remembered his good friend Konrad. A brilliant mathematician, always looking for excitement and craving adventure, he would embrace the war and relish the danger. And Patryk. A year older than himself and a brilliant horseman, who without a second thought had signed up to join the cavalry. Was he still alive? There had been such terrible rumours circulating. Were any true? There was no way of knowing.

Everyone had heard of the bravery of the Polish cavalry. On 1 September 1939, the very first day of the invasion, their traditional charge had successfully dispersed a German infantry battalion a few miles from Krojanty. But moments later they had been surrounded by armoured cars that had approached unseen from the nearby forest, armed with machine guns. Completely exposed in the clearing the cavalry had been forced to gallop for cover – horses' hooves thudding on the hard ground, churning the earth into large clods that flayed the air as they frantically raced for cover from the murderous crossfire. Almost a third of the cavalry had been killed or wounded that day.

Saddened by the memories, he tried to shut them out, but deep down he knew that one of his best friends was dead. Tears welled up in his eyes and angrily he brushed them away. No one must see him cry; he was a soldier and mustn't show any sign of weakness. But in the still and quiet of the night, he knew he wasn't the only one who remembered fallen comrades.

'This will be your grave.' The commandant's words came back to haunt Vadek as he lay there, but he forced himself to blank them out. Wrapping his blanket tightly round him, he began to drift to another place in a different time … a kinder time … and in the foggy realms of half-sleep he could once again hear his mother calling …

TWO

KAPICE-LIPNIKI, NEAR BIALYSTOK, NORTH-EASTERN POLAND: SEPTEMBER 1929

IT WAS IN FREIGHT CARS WE CAME FROM THE EAST, FIGHTING FOR A SACRED CAUSE, WE SHALL NOT CEASE.

POLISH SOLDIERS, ITALY 1944

'Vadek, Vadek! … Where are you?' Camilla Kossakowski stood on the top step at the open doorway and looked around the farmyard for her ten-year-old son. Her weathered, smiling face was framed by a faded, cotton scarf holding back her fair hair, and she held a basket in one hand and a large metal pail in the other.

In the woodshed, Vadek was sitting on a pile of logs with a look of intense concentration on his face. In one hand, a small but well sharpened knife whittled away at a piece of wood which was now beginning to resemble a stork: one of the many that nested on the chimneys during the late spring. Watching these birds standing on only one spindly leg, motionless for hours, Vadek always wondered how it was they never fell over, as he and his friends could never manage more than a few minutes, balancing shakily, arms waving, before they collapsed.

'*VADEK!!*' The call came again, more insistent and louder this time, and he knew he could no longer get away with pretending he hadn't heard. Sighing, he placed his carving on a log, yelling that he was coming. Then he sprinted across the farmyard to where his mother was waiting.

'Will you collect the eggs for me?' she asked him, handing him the basket. 'I'm just going to fetch more water. And don't drop any, mind,' she added as he ran off towards the chicken house.

That child's always in a hurry, she thought fondly as she made her way to the well. Her ghostly face stared up at her in the water as she turned the handle, and shattered as she lowered the bucket into its dark depths.

Vadek, bending low through the doorway of the chicken house and stooping once inside, pushed the hens from their nests and carefully placed each egg onto the cloth in the basket.

'Stupid chickens,' he muttered as one bird jumped onto his head, her claws scratching his head, while another landed on his back. 'You should be used to this by now – I come every day.' By the time he had finished, there were quite a few feathers lying around and several irate hens squawking. Then proudly clutching the basket in front of him, he made his way back to the house, convinced he'd got the better of the hens this time – and not one broken egg!

His mother was stoking the large cast-iron stove that dominated the kitchen; she straightened when he entered, and he watched the flames flicker around the logs before she closed the door. Potatoes, newly dug from the nearby field, were boiling on top, and the kettle was steaming, as Camilla told him to wash before dinner.

The kitchen was the largest and busiest room, the heart of the home. It was also the warmest – sometimes unbearably so during the summer – but Vadek was glad of its heat when the long, cold months of the Polish winter set in. Then a blanket of snow would cover the ground, hard and crisp in the sub-zero temperatures, and the frost would form traceable patterns on the window-panes.

He liked the winter evenings, when they would all sit in the warmth of the stove, the oil lamp throwing their shadows on the walls and ceiling. He and his father would play with the chess set his father had made for him one Christmas, and his mother would tell him folk stories – hopefully his favourite one, about Krakus, a warrior from Krakow who slew a dragon with the help of his mystical stallion. The family would sing songs; there were so many rousing Polish songs, but those that told heroic stories were ones he liked the best.

But now it was late summer and there was much to do for the winter. His father was busy in the fields every day till late, often coming in when Vadek was asleep and leaving again before dawn.

Pouring some water into a bowl, Vadek splashed his face and scrubbed his hands before sitting himself down at the table. He reached for a chunk of the dark rye bread his mother had baked that morning, but before he could start eating – for as usual he was ravenously hungry – he had to wait for his father to come in. Suddenly the door opened, letting in a large blast of cold air against the heat of the kitchen.

His father's lined face was brown as leather and his blue eyes twinkled from under his frayed cloth cap. A man of few words, he had worked on the land all his life, taking on the farm after his father and his father's father before him, and so it had always been for many generations. At one time, the Kossakowskis had been noblemen, with a coat of arms, and landowners, providing employment and a livelihood for many people on their great estates; but over the centuries their land – and hence their wealth and power – had been eroded, confiscated by different political regimes. Now there were only a few fields they could call their own. And it was all so long ago that few remembered.

Czeslav stomped his boots on the doormat then pulled out a chair and sat down opposite his son. Camilla placed a large mug of steaming black tea in front of him and, cupping it in his large, coarse hands with their faint odour of horsehair and hay, he looked directly at Vadek,

'I think it's about time you came along with me and learnt how to handle the old horse and plough.'

He paused to take a large swallow of his tea: 'Tomorrow will do just fine.'

Then picking up his spoon he proceeded to eat his dinner of cabbage and potato pancakes with great gusto, finishing it in just a few mouthfuls. Wiping his sleeve across his mouth, he gulped down the rest of his tea before giving Vadek a fond pat on the head, ruffling his hair. Then with a nod of thanks to his wife, he was off outside again.

Early the following morning in the pre-dawn light, before the cockerel had raised his voice to greet the sunrise, Vadek roused himself. His father had already gone out and, quickly dressing, Vadek made his way to the kitchen where his mother was lighting the stove.

With a cheerful greeting and pulling on his warm jacket and boots, he left the house, jumping down the three steps in one bound before running across the yard to the cowshed. As he pushed open the door she turned, staring at him with her large, lustrous eyes and gave a loud moo, her breath warm and sweet in contrast to the chilly air outside.

Vadek made himself comfortable on the little three-legged milking stool and placed the pail in position beneath her. She barely stirred as he warmed his hands under his jacket before, with a friendly pat on the cow's back, he began milking.

A year or two ago, it had taken him a fair bit of practice to get any results, but now he found it a pleasant enough job and would whistle a soft tune as he rhythmically squeezed her udders, for she was a gentle thing and Vadek had grown fond of her.

When the pail was full, he gave her some fresh hay and another pat before he left the warmth of the barn and carried the milk into the house. His usual breakfast of bread and warm milk was ready for him.

'Be quick now, or you'll be late for school,' his mother said as she broke off a large piece of rye bread and wrapped it in a muslin cloth for his lunch. School started at 7.30 am sharp and Vadek had nearly a three-mile walk.

Finishing his meal, he pulled his hat well down over his ears, then wrapped his scarf around his jacket and head to keep out the brisk winds that blew across the open fields.

'On your way, then,' said his mother, 'and no dawdling.'

Then, pushing an apple into his pocket while giving him a quick hug, she watched as he crossed the farmyard, passed the outbuildings and turned into the lane. With a wave goodbye, Vadek sauntered along the dusty dirt track to his cousin Andrzei's house, already biting into his apple. The weather was becoming colder; there was a distinct autumnal feel in the air and the wind pinched his cheeks and bit his fingers as it rustled the fallen leaves along the ground. He could see Andrzei waiting for him, leaning against the weathered picket fence at the front of the farmhouse. Munching on the seeds picked from the sunflowers that grew in abundance along the lane, Andrzei pinged some at Vadek, calling him to hurry: '*Chodz na! Chodz na!*'

Andrzei was tall and wiry with a shock of bright red hair and freckles. His great-grandmother on his father's side had been English, and he had been the only one in the family to inherit her colouring; something he wasn't very happy about, for he stuck out like a sore thumb amongst the other children. Now twelve, he would soon be leaving the tiny Catholic school at the neighbouring village of Jezewo – with its nine children – for the much larger boarding school in Suwalki, many miles distant. His older brother Pavel was already there and so was only at home during the holidays.

Laughing, Vadek ran to catch Andrzei up, and together they ran several hundred yards more before pausing for breath and continuing at a slower pace to the cottage where their friends Tadek and Henja were waiting.

The walk took the four across fields by the river. It was peaceful, with only a farmer to be seen herding his cows to the river to drink. Occasionally a stork would sweep down, low and graceful, over the meadows in search of a field mouse or shrew to take home to its young.

Henja, a slight, fair-haired five-year-old, had started school earlier that year and was the youngest there. On the walk she had trouble keeping up with the pace set by the older boys, so Andrzei would carry her on his back for as long as he could. He didn't like school much and wasn't particularly bothered whether he learnt anything or not, eagerly awaiting midday when the bell would ring to end the lessons for that day.

They covered the distance by playing tag or singing. Their songs excited the dogs in the farmyards and they would run out after them yapping and jumping at their heels as they passed. This would make Henja scream, and the children would run off shouting and laughing.

'It's because you can't sing,' Vadek teased Andrzei, and ran off, throwing his apple core at his head.

'More likely because you smell!' Andrzei retorted and raced off after him, flinging himself at him in a rugby tackle so they both went down, rolling around together.

'Come on you two, or we'll be late,' grumbled eleven-year-old Tadek, always the more serious one – but even he couldn't help grinning at their antics sometimes as they hurried on their way.

Today, school couldn't finish quickly enough for Vadek, and his teacher had to warn him more than once to pay attention. Vadek was of course hoping that his father hadn't forgotten his promise to let him plough the field, for it wasn't often he had the chance to spend so much time in his father's company.

Rushing out as soon as the bell rang, he sprinted in front of the others and only Andrzei could keep up.

'I've never seen you run so fast,' his cousin complained, gasping for breath and leaning heavily against the fence as they reached his home. Shouting goodbye, Vadek ran the rest of the way, panting so hard he could barely stand up as he burst through the door.

His mother was busy in the kitchen. 'My goodness!' she exclaimed, 'Where's the fire?' Wiping her hands on her apron, she fetched him a drink she had made from their own apples and smiled as Vadek gulped it greedily.

'Don't you remember? Father promised to let me plough the field today,' he explained between gulps, 'and I didn't want to miss him.'

'Well, I hope you have enough energy left to be of use to me,' remarked his father, coming into the room and smiling when he saw his son's flushed face.

'Oh, I have lots!' Vadek answered. 'You'll see, you'll have trouble keeping up with me!'

With a laugh, Czeslav sniffed appreciatively. 'Mmmm … I thought I could smell something good,' he said eyeing the tray of freshly baked *pączki*. Helping himself to three of them, he handed one to Vadek, who beamed on accepting his favourite treat.

'Oww! Theve are gffreat,' he mumbled through a mouthful, 'but they sure are hot!!'

'Now you know why I married your mother!' his father said as he finished his second doughnut with a satisfied smile to his wife. Then wiping his mouth on his sleeve and pulling his cap back on, he turned to Vadek, saying, 'Now, we have work to do.'

Together they strode over to the barn. Inside, the large workhorse was chomping away at the hay but turned with a whiffle of welcome as they entered. Reaching the harness down from its hook, Czeslav showed his son how to arrange it over the horse's back, all the time talking softly to him, for he was a kind man who believed a gentle touch was better than a harsh word and if you wanted to get the best from an animal you treated it well.

Vadek watched intently, for he knew that a mistake in fitting the harness could cause an accident. When all was ready, with a click of his teeth Czeslav led the horse out of the barn and to the field where the plough was stored. As they attached him to the harness, Vadek heard a shout and someone calling his name. Looking up, he saw his cousin and his uncle already at work in the opposite field, and he waved at them, grinning broadly.

The horse knew his job well for he had been ploughing the fields for many years, and so he would wait patiently when Vadek faltered in the mud, and would turn without guidance at the end of each furrow.

Vadek's face was set in deep concentration as he stumbled along behind horse and plough, his eyes following each furrow as he tried to keep a straight line. Gritting his teeth, he did not notice the wind harsh in his face, nor his fingers stiffening around the reins. Nor the clods that spattered up, hitting his face and hair, as the plough broke into the earth, filling the air with the smell of fresh earth as it overturned the clumps of grass. It had seemed so easy when he had watched Andrzei or his father do it; just walking steadily behind the horse in a straight line. Nothing to it, he had thought – but he was wrong.

It was difficult, strenuous work and by the time a third of the field had been completed, he was really feeling the strain of physically trying to coordinate the movement of such a strong animal with the heavy plough, combined with the intense concentration it required. But his father was pleased and patted him on the back saying what a great farmer he would make.

Vadek tried not to show how thankful he was when his father at last said it was becoming too dark to do any more, and his mouth curved into a smile when he realised it was Sunday the following day, with no school and no work!

The following morning dawned bright and clear with the first frost of the autumn. All the family slept in on a Sunday; even the cow had to wait to be milked. After a breakfast of leftovers from yesterday's supper accompanied by warm bread and jam, Vadek's father dressed in his only suit – the one he had worn when he had married Camilla. It was a little worn at the edges with a patch on one elbow, but still smart enough to be seen in for the local church service. Vadek, too, wore his best clothes, and was very proud of the new woollen shirt his mother had woven for him. With Camilla wearing her best hat of turquoise blue – to match her eyes, her husband said – they were ready to leave for the Sunday Mass at the Catholic church in Jezewo, not far from the village school.

Czeslav harnessed the horse to the cart and Vadek sat next to him on the driver's perch, with his mother in the back. Then with a click of his tongue and a flick of the reins, they bumped along the track to Andrzei's house.

'*Dzien dobry! Dzien dobry!*' His uncle welcomed them in his usual boom as he pulled his frame up with a groan and squeezed it onto the seat in the cart, followed by his aunt. Accompanying them as always were Andrzei's grandmother and grandfather, and somehow they all managed to wedge themselves in, leaving Andrzei to climb up next to Vadek and his father.

Once everyone was settled they were on their way again, the horse plodding along through the countryside.

Along the way they passed the house of Jakub, a man of Jewish descent, and his son Jerzy. Pausing from tending the vegetable patch, they both leaned on their spades to wave and shout a greeting.

'That reminds me,' said Camilla thoughtfully, 'I must bring some eggs for them and maybe some jam too.'

'So how did the ploughing go yesterday?' Andrzei asked Vadek. 'Bet you didn't finish the whole field.'

'Oh, it was easy,' claimed Vadek, stealing a glance at his father, who couldn't quite hold back a smile as he innocently clicked at the horse. 'Well, erm, maybe it was a little bit more difficult than I'd thought.'

Andrzei dug him in the ribs. 'Don't worry about it, squirt,' he said. 'Everyone thinks it's an easy job till they do it. I know I did.' Pulling up his sleeve and he proudly flexing his arm, he said, 'Look, keep it up and you'll soon have muscles like mine.'

Vadek wasn't impressed: 'Well, I hope I'll have better ones than that.' Andrzei pulled Vadek's cap over his face.

The church was the one where Czeslav and Camilla had been married some years before. As it was the only one for many miles, at services it was full to overflowing and everyone seemed to know everyone else. Tadek and Henja were there with their parents, and the Kossakowskis joined them, squashing up close together in their pew to the indignation of the other churchgoers already seated. The service was always in Latin, which none of the children could understand and they had to be told not to fidget as time wore on.

Once outside again everyone milled around chatting about nothing in particular, just passing the time of day and talking to people they only saw on Sundays. This was a good excuse for Vadek and his friends to meet with other children from their school, and play chase or hide and seek amongst the trees until it was time to leave. Ana, a girl from a neighbouring village would often join in, but would usually prance off in a huff when Andrzei tweaked one of her plaits.

Usually, Andrzei's family would continue to Vadek's house and while the women prepared dinner, the men folk sat idly, discussing the general work on the farm or debating the topical matters of the time. Sometimes Vadek and Andrzei played chess; but Vadek was by far the better player – and Andrzei being a poor loser, would bring his clenched fist down on the table with a resounding thump and demand a rematch.

Vadek rarely became agitated over anything and would have trouble trying to stifle his laughter over Andrzei's sudden bursts of temper; but just as suddenly as he flared up, Andrzei could simmer down again. His outbursts never lasted long and were forgotten almost instantly.

'I blame his red hair,' his mother would say with a knowing look: 'Red hair, hot temper.'

Bringing some apples, fresh bread, cold meats and jam to share, everyone would gather round the kitchen table and noisily enjoy the best meal of the week. This would usually start with tomatoes thinly sliced and liberally covered with salt and black pepper, sliced pork or ham from the pigs at Tadek's small farm and thick chunks of fresh rye bread in a large bowl in the middle of the table for everyone to help themselves.

Then would come *bigos*, a traditional dish of spicy smoked sausage and cabbage, served hot with boiled potatoes, to be followed by *szarlotka*, apple cake – or Vadek's favourite, *pączki*. The room would be filled with the aroma of good food and the sound of voices talking excitedly over one another.

As the afternoon passed into the quiet of evening, Andrzei's grandfather would tell a story. To Vadek, he seemed as old as time itself. His face had the texture of ancient parchment but his eyes sparkled and his face became animated as he brought a story to life.

He told stories that had been retold over the centuries, so old that no-one knew their origin, of the storks that nested on the chimneys or the white-tipped eagles that lived on the crags of the high Tatras in southern Poland. Then sometimes they would sing songs about Polish kings or of Polish generals such as Henryk Dabrowski, who had fought with Napoleon against the Tartars.

Andrzei especially loved hearing of the heroic battles of the Winged Hussars, a Polish cavalry unit famed for their huge wings, wooden frames attached to their backs with brilliantly coloured eagle and goose feathers arching high over their heads. What a wondrous sight they must have been; surely the sight alone was enough to deter any enemy! But it was not just for show; their technical brilliance and their courage gave them victory in battle after battle. It was always the battle of Vienna in 1683 which never failed to get Andrzei out of his seat. Grabbing whatever came to hand, usually a ladle or some other item of cutlery, he would pretend it was a sabre and wave it madly this way and that while jumping from one chair to another, making everyone in the room duck quickly, hoping they were not in the way of Andrzei the dashing cavalry officer.

But as the years wore on, the friendly chatter would take on a more serious note with talk concerning the state of their homeland and neighbouring countries – especially about Germany, which bordered Poland on the west and its new chancellor, who came to power in 1933.

A man by the name of Adolf Hitler.

THREE

KAPICE, SEPTEMBER 1931

THE POLISH ARMY HAS THE BEST INTELLIGENCE IN THE WORLD. ITS VALUE FOR US IS PRICELESS. UNFORTUNATELY, WE CANNOT OFFER MUCH IN RETURN.

GENERAL KRONER, DEPUTY CHIEF
OF US MILITARY INTELLIGENCE, 1944

Vadek now had a brother, Roman, a chubby boy with rosy cheeks and an angelic smile that belied his nature. He adored his big brother and followed him wherever he went, toddling after Vadek whether he wanted him to or not.

Andrzei had been attending the school in Suwalki for the past two years and Vadek had missed him. But now the time had come for Vadek too to go to boarding school, leaving all that he knew. It was a daunting prospect for a twelve-year-old, and Vadek had been filled with mixed apprehension and anticipation.

His father had readied the horse and cart for the fifteen-mile ride to the railway station just outside the market town of Bialystok. From there, Vadek had a six-hour train journey to his destination.

The sky was overcast with the promise of rain to come, and dirt blew up from the yard in front of the house. Vadek's mother smiled, holding back the tears. Her hair was tied back, but tendrils blew across her face. She hugged him tightly then pushed a white muslin cloth into his hand.

'Bread and ham,' she explained, 'for the journey, and of course a *pączek*.'

Vadek's father lifted his son's canvas bag into the cart. 'Come on,' he said, 'we must leave now; the train won't wait,' and pulled himself onto the seat, clasping the reins in his hands.

Vadek swung Roman into the air with a low grunt, not realising how heavy he was, and hugged him close.

'Goodbye little brother, I'll see you at Christmas.'

Then he climbed up onto the seat next to his father. With a flick of the reins and a click of his tongue, his father encouraged the horse to break into a trot. Turning, Vadek gave a final wave and a shout goodbye – but at this Roman seemed to realise that he wasn't going to go along too, and broke into a run, shouting for Vadek at the top of his voice. Camilla ran after her younger son, soon catching him and clutching his hand tightly in hers; they watched until the cart had disappeared in a cloud of dust. Vadek could hear Roman's yells long after they were out of sight.

'For such a little fellow, he certainly has a large pair of lungs,' commented his father with a smile, trying to instil some humour into a rather sombre occasion.

When they arrived at the railway station, some large drops of rain began to fall. Jumping down from the cart with his bag, Vadek turned rather awkwardly to his father, who had also got down.

'Well son, this is it; work hard and do your best, no one can expect any more,' Czeslav advised briskly, his face impassive, trying to conceal his emotions. Grasping Vadek's hand in his, he shook it firmly, then with a reassuring pat on his son's back he climbed back onto the cart. With a shake on the reins and without looking back, he moved off, the wheels clattering on the cobblestones.

Rather forlornly, Vadek stood there; a small and solitary figure watching until his father was well out of sight. Then he turned his attention to what was happening around him. Slowly he made his way to the platform where a train was standing. It was Saturday, market day in Bialystok, a town larger than Jezewo and Kapice put together. People came from neighbouring villages and farms to either buy or sell their produce or animals; it was here that Czeslav had purchased their chickens and workhorse several years before.

There were squealing pigs in carts, squawking chickens in crates in wheelbarrows, and farmers herding their cows with a swish of a cane on their rumps; trying to keep them in some sort of order as they ambled out of the trucks. Everyone was going to the central market place. Everywhere was bustling with noise and movement with throngs of people calling out to one another or yelling at their animals. The strangeness of it all was overwhelming, and Vadek felt a little lost and overawed.

He was startled by a blast of steam and a belch of smoke as with a churning of pistons, the driver indicated that he was ready to leave. Jumping on board as the train began to move, Vadek found a seat next to the window. The carriages were cold and draughty with wooden benches to sit on. Luckily, there were more people arriving for the start of the market than departing, so the train was practically empty.

There was one other occupant in his compartment; an old peasant woman, her leathery brown face partly covered by a rather grubby woollen shawl. She was carrying a tattered canvas bag full of potatoes and holding on tightly to a very flustered plump hen which clearly took objection to its surroundings, clucking noisily as the train rattled along. As the train pulled away from the station, Vadek turned his attention to the view outside the window. Green open fields were moving past, dotted here and there with farmhouses not unlike his own. Despite the rain, people were toiling in the fields, digging up vegetables to be taken to market later that day, and occasionally he saw a farmer ploughing his field – just like he would be doing at home, he thought with a sudden pang of emotion.

He was glad of the lunch his mother had made for him, but once he had finished it, there was nothing to do except sleep. He closed his eyes and, wooden seat notwithstanding, probably would have nodded off if the train, for no reason that he could think of, hadn't kept jerking to stops and starts.

Eventually, the countryside gave way to buildings. Vadek had arrived at Suwalki. He pushed down the window and stuck his head out, and heard a loud yell of recognition above the hissing of the train and clanging of doors. Andrzei had started the new term a few days earlier and had come to the station to meet him. Vadek's face broke into a huge grin for it was so wonderful to see a familiar face. He gave a shout and waved madly, and Andrzei ran up and pulled open the carriage door. Vadek grabbed his bag as Andrzei yanked him from the train and gave him a thump on the back.

'So you're here at last, I've been waiting ages,' he said. Vadek told him about the train stopping and starting.

'Oh, that's nothing, it always does that,' he said. 'I think it would be faster to go by horse and cart!'

The clouds had lifted and the late afternoon sun was breaking through as they made their way out of the station to walk the last couple of miles to the school. All the while Andrzei talked nonstop, trying to fill Vadek in with all the details about the school.

'I'll only be able to see you on Sundays at church, as we're not allowed to mix with the first formers or go to other dormitories,' he explained, 'but don't worry; you'll soon make friends. There's lots of others starting today too, so you're not the only one – but it's a lot different from Jezewo, you know!'

He paused for breath before continuing. 'The teachers are very strict,' he warned, 'and watch you like a hawk. There's no talking allowed in class or at Sunday Mass; only after mealtimes and when lessons have finished.'

He smiled at Vadek's now rather anxious face. 'Don't worry, the food's good … look, here we are,' and as they approached a pair of large wrought-iron gates with a coat of arms on one of them, he gave a wide sweep of his arm and announced grandly, 'Your new home.'

As they passed through the gates and walked along the drive, Vadek gazed around him in some bewilderment. The lengthening evening shadows reached across the lawns that stretched immaculately before him – and there, right in the centre of them, was his new school.

It was certainly an impressive building, of dull red brick with two floors set in a square around a central paved courtyard. Vadek's eyes followed the ornate white brickwork that ran along the top to the onion-shaped domes at each of the four corners, the last rays of the dying sun glinting in the Gothic windows and giving a golden hue to the brick. It reminded him of castles belonging to Polish kings which he had seen only in books. Maybe a king had even lived here, he thought to himself.

'It's a bit big,' he said in hushed tones, then pulled himself up sharply. Why was he whispering?

Andrzei slipped a reassuring arm over his shoulders. 'Don't worry, I felt like that at first; it does rather hit you doesn't it?' He gave a short laugh. 'Nothing like back home is it?'

Vadek remembered the friendly little timber-built school at Jezewo, with its single room for all the children, despite their different ages. 'It certainly isn't,' he agreed slowly.

FOUR

SUWALKI, SEPTEMBER 1931

**THE RUSSIANS WILL SWEEP THROUGH YOUR
COUNTRY, AND YOUR PEOPLE WILL BE LIQUIDATED.
YOU ARE ON THE VERGE OF ANNIHILATION.**

WINSTON CHURCHILL, 14 OCTOBER 1944

Vadek's first few days passed in a blur, for there was just so much to take in. With different lessons in different rooms, often some distance from each other and even stairs leading to yet more rooms on another floor, it was all very confusing, and he had trouble finding where he was supposed to be. 'I need a map' he grumbled to himself as yet again he was lost in the maze of corridors and late for his lesson.

There were new subjects too: Latin, astronomy and physics, along with the usual mathematics, science, history, German, Italian and, of course, Polish. At least he didn't have a problem with rising at five in the morning for prayers in the school chapel, though after the peace of his small room at home in Kapice it took him a while to get accustomed to the snoring from some of the other boys in the dormitory. A horrid thought crossed his mind … he might snore too! And Andrzei was right, the food was good. Very often he would see his cousin at meal times, but they were not permitted to talk, and could only nod to each other.

With so much studying, Vadek had little time to reflect on his position. However, when the lights were out at 8pm and all was quiet except for the steady breathing of the fifteen other boys in his dormitory, he would feel a surge of homesickness, for then his thoughts turned to his family and the friends he had left behind.

In the hour before lights out they were free to do what they pleased: reading, studying, or just relaxing. It was then that Vadek wrote to his family and read their letters. He especially liked the drawings that Roman would scrawl in coloured pencils of the farm or the storks and matchstick figures of his mother and father and himself.

On Saturdays there were classes only in the morning but the compulsory physical training in the afternoon was not something Vadek enjoyed at all; anything that didn't occupy the mind he would find boring and see as a waste of time. The PT disciplines would vary from high jump and sprinting to running on the spot or jumping up and down vigorously while clapping hands above the head. More often than not, this would cause him to break into a fit of giggles as he could picture Roman, trying so hard to emulate his older brother and falling over in the process.

Sundays was the only day with no lessons at all, and after church the rest of the day was theirs to do as they pleased. Usually he met up with Andrzei, and sometimes joined in a game of friendly football if the weather was fine – though he would usually end up as goalkeeper, hoping the ball wouldn't come too close. More often than not, when it did his mind was elsewhere. so he would miss it. Andrzei would berate him but Vadek would laugh, for he could never get that passionate about sport. This, unsurprisingly, made Andrzei feel even more angry and frustrated, but despite it all they remained good friends.

The library on the top floor was always open. It overlooked the grounds and you could expect to find Vadek sitting in the window seat, the rays of the evening sun highlighting his hair as he sat in peaceful solitude, soaking up books about places in the world he had never even heard of before, in the hope one day of seeing some of them.

As he wrote in his letters to his mother, although the teachers were indeed very strict, the time passed pleasantly enough and school was pretty good; once you got used to it.

JULY 1932

It was early morning and the sun's warm fingers had yet to creep over the horizon as Vadek banged loudly on the door of his cousin's dormitory shouting impatiently. '*Chodz na! Andrzei!*'

The door opened slowly and Andrzei's tousled red head peered it round blearily. 'What's all the commotion, little cousin?' he muttered drowsily, brushing his hair back. 'What's happening?'

'Nothing if you don't get a move on fast,' Vadek replied, pushing open the door. 'Don't you know what time it is?'

'Yeah, time I went back to sleep,' Andrzei mumbled as he flopped back down on his bed. 'Come back later, at a more reasonable time.'

'You DON'T know what time it is!' said Vadek. 'We have a train to catch in less than an hour!'

Andrzei shot upright. 'What! Why didn't you wake me?'

It was the last day of term. In the year that had passed, Vadek had changed from a quiet boy into a confident teenager. But although he was now used to being away from home, he couldn't wait to see his family again. He grabbed Andrzei's things and began shoving them into his bag while his cousin dressed. 'Where's my shoe?' Andrzei cried, hopping about on one foot while pulling on a sock at the same time.

'Here, you idiot!' said Vadek, throwing it at him. 'Now, get a move on!'

Andrzei ducked, then cramming his feet into his shoes, grabbed his belongings and fairly flew out of the door and down the corridor. 'Let's go!' he yelled.

Vadek dashed out after him and together they raced across the grounds, out through the gates and into the near-deserted streets towards the railway station. With only the one train leaving for Bialystok early that morning, they couldn't afford to miss it.

With only seconds to spare, they flung themselves into a compartment as the train pulled away from the platform. Laughing and panting, they slung their bags on the floor and collapsed onto the nearest bench.

'Hooray!' Andrzei shouted, throwing his cap in the air. 'No more school. No more Latin. Who needs it anyway? I can never understand it.' He reached over and knocked Vadek's cap off. 'I'm going to join the army.'

'You'll never get up in time,' said Vadek, 'They'll have you up so early you won't have time to go to bed.'

Laughing, the two cousins settled back and watched as Suwalki made way for the countryside and farmlands they knew so well.

The long, hot summer days with their cooler, more pleasant evenings passed far too quickly. Days were spent playing with friends, swimming in the river and of course working on the farm, for it was late summer and harvest time.

Haymaking was something that took several days and involved a great deal of work. The hay was cut manually with a scythe, then raked into rows the length of the meadow before being raked into large piles to be pitchforked onto the cart as it passed slowly along each row. This was something everyone enjoyed doing and neighbouring farmers came to help, for it was also a time to talk and discuss their yields while sharing produce.

Andrzei and his father would be there, Tadek with Henja, Ana, and Jerzy with his father, Jakub. Even little Roman, now almost five, would help by gathering the hay into piles. However, he would then dive, yelling and kicking, into the bundles, scattering the hay into the air, so was more of a hindrance than a help; but he looked so comical with his hair and clothes bristling with hay that no-one seemed to mind.

As the hay was piled higher in the cart, Vadek and Andrzei would jump on top and grab the hay as it was pitched up. This meant they rose higher and higher, risking falling off as the cart lurched along. When no more hay could be balanced on the tottering pile, the cart would trundle back to the barn, where the hay was unloaded to be stored in the loft, ready for winter.

When the last of the hay had been loaded and stored, the sun would be low in the sky. Tired and hungry, the haymakers would amble over to the meadow where Camilla, Ana and Henja would bring them plates of salt pork, ham and smoked sausage, bread and eggs. Always eager to talk and eat, they would keep up a lively conversation until well into the evening until it was almost too dark to see, the mosquitoes were biting and Roman had fallen asleep curled up on his mother's lap.

The river was a magnet for all the local children. The older boys would dive in and have races, while the younger ones and less confident would jump about in the shallows, splashing each other wildly. It had been one of those glorious days that heralded the end of the summer and now it was a perfect evening, a mild breeze rustling the grass, swallows circling the meadows and dragonflies hovering low over the water.

Vadek was stretched out on the cool grass, resting after a swim. Henja was plaiting a necklace with the wild flowers that adorned the riverbank, focusing on each stem as she threaded one end into the end of another. Tadek was lying nearby with a long stem of grass between his teeth. Vadek, eyes closed, looked asleep but was working on a mathematical problem that was part of his homework and oblivious to his surroundings.

Tadek nudged his sister and silently mouthed her to be quiet as he took the grass from his mouth and poked it gently into Vadek's ear. Henja suppressed a giggle as she watched Vadek absent-mindedly raise a hand to brush the fly away. Tadek leaned nearer and softly stroked Vadek's nose with the fronds. Vadek wrinkled his nose and screwed up his face, brushing the grass away in annoyance, making Henja squeal and Tadek roll over laughing. Vadek opened his eyes in surprise and his mouth to speak, when suddenly a scream pierced the air. Everyone stopped what they doing and looked around.

It had come from further along the river and people, hesitant at first, started to run towards where they thought it had come from. Vadek sat up, looking in the direction of the sound as did the others, all wondering what was happening. For a few timeless seconds they remained motionless, then scrambling up Vadek started to run, shouting urgently for Tadek to follow. Ordering his sister to stay where she was, Tadek sprinted to catch up with his friend.

A small group of people had gathered a short distance away, some were crying but most stood in shock, unable to accept what they were seeing. Vadek pushed through and pressed forward, then stopped and watched in horror as a body was dragged from the water. Tadek silently joined him. As they stood there, Henja came running up panting, and pulled at her brother's arm, loudly complaining at being left behind. Vadek turned to her sharply, snapping at her to be quiet. Henja gaped at him, shocked by his tone; Tadek took her hand, gently leading her away from the scene. Vadek, stunned, abruptly turned and dazedly walked away, shaken. For it was a classmate, a partner in science lessons, and a friend, killed by diving into a too-shallow part of the river and breaking his neck. Vadek was deeply saddened and it affected him profoundly, for he had been unable to help his friend, and for the remainder of the summer he avoided the river.

JULY, 1933

'Got you! Got you!' Andrzei cried, jumping about triumphantly. 'A direct hit, a bullet in the brain! You're dead!' He paused. 'Well, go on then. Lie down and die!' he ordered.

'No, no, I'm not dead, only wounded,' protested Vadek. 'I don't die that easily.'

They were playing in the forest which bordered the furthest fields of the farms. It was a favourite haunt of theirs in the holidays. With them were Tadek and Henja, for though she was a mere girl, as Andrzei bluntly remarked, two people were needed on each side to make it fair. As long as, of course, she wasn't on *his* side.

It was a warm summer evening; a gentle breeze fanned their faces, and the chirping of the crickets could be heard over the children's voices. After several attempts, the four had successfully lashed some branches together to make a base, interweaving some broader, leafier ones to make a roof.

Perfect, they had all agreed at last, standing back to admire their work. Camouflaged as it was, it made a perfect hideaway and an excellent base for the war games they were playing. They were soldiers, shooting at the enemy with 'rifle' branches. This was Andrzei's favourite game; rather unfairly, he always demanded that he should win. But this time the enemy – Henja and Vadek – refused to die without putting up a stiff fight.

'Okay, okay, I'll let you live if you surrender,' Andrzei condescended ungracefully.

'No way!' shouted Vadek, 'Come on Henja – let's get 'em!' Undaunted and with a loud yell, he charged straight at Andrzei and Tadek, while Henja carried out a surprise attack from the rear, grabbing fallen pine cones and throwing them as fast and as hard as she could. 'Grenades away!' she cried, as a direct hit caught Tadek on the chin.

'Hey!' he protested, 'I'm your brother!'

'Not now, you're not,' she replied with yet another direct hit to his head. 'You're the enemy!'

'I'm glad you're on my side, Henja,' said Vadek, then ducked as a cone whizzed by his ear, catching Andrzei full on the nose. Rubbing it ruefully, Andrzei admitted defeat, especially in the face of Henja's determined look as she threatened him with another 'grenade'.

'Maybe girls should be allowed to join the army after all,' said Tadek, giving Andrzei a push.

The evening sun filtered through the pines and their sweet smell lingered in the air as the children sat amicably on some tree stumps munching sunflower seeds and chatting. Then talk turned to Andrzei's older brother, Pavel; now seventeen, he was a cadet in the Polish army in Warsaw, and would write thrilling letters home detailing how he was learning to drive the 7TP Czolg Lekki. These were the newly designed light Polish tanks, and Andrzei would pore over his letters with great excitement, for it all seemed such a wonderful experience to him and so very different from boring old farmwork. Such was his eagerness, he could rarely talk of anything else, hoping fervently to be in charge of his own tank; for him, the time could not come quickly enough.

FIVE

CAMP KOLA, APRIL 1940

IT'S A MATTER OF INDIFFERENCE TO ME, WHAT A WEAK WESTERN EUROPEAN CIVILISATION WILL SAY ABOUT ME.

ADOLF HITLER, AUGUST 1939

Vadek could not sleep. He was exhausted. His body cried out for sleep, but he was too cold. A numb gnawing cold, which penetrated deep into the bones with such an intensity that it became a physical pain the like of which he had never experienced before but now was his constant companion. He huddled under the worn blanket, wearing all his clothes including his hat and what was left of his gloves. His socks had disintegrated many months ago, his boots were falling apart and his toes were dark with frostbite. He did not know how much longer he could survive. Did he want to survive? All too often he wanted to succumb to the sleep he would not awaken from; to break free from this terrible never-ending nightmare. Alive but not living. Daily he walked side by side with death, for it was his only friend.

He willed himself to focus on pleasant thoughts; searching for memories which seemed a lifetime away … he would not allow himself to forget. He could not forget. Because the memories were all that kept him sane.

Back at Kapice in spring 1928, the countryside was awakening from winter's grip. Pale green shoots were pushing their way through the ground and a few early tiny buds sprouted from the tips of the branches on bushes and trees.

The chores were all done for the day and the nine-year-old Vadek was finishing his potato pancakes in much less time than it had taken his mother to make them.

'I'll be off out then,' he declared, pushing his empty plate away and rising from the table. 'Tadek's moving their pigs today and I promised to help.'

'That'll keep you out of mischief,' commented his father, 'but watch out for the old sow; she doesn't take to being moved. Too set in her ways, like me.'

'Wait a moment – take these with you,' and Camilla pushed two bruised apples deep into his jacket pockets as she handed it to him, making them bulge out awkwardly. 'And here's one for *you*, before you ask,' she said. 'Those are for the pigs.'

'Do they like apples, then?' asked Vadek, taking a bite while shrugging his shoulders into his now tight jacket.

'Oh yes,' said Czeslav, with a knowing wink at his wife. 'You'll be glad of those apples right enough; once they smell them, they'll follow you anywhere. That's if you don't eat them first.'

Although the days were becoming warmer, a stiff breeze blew across the open fields as Vadek ran along the dirt track to Tadek's house. He could see Andrzei with Tadek, and Ana was there as well, talking to Henja who was swinging on the gate. On seeing him, Henja gave a wave and shouted, 'Hurry up! We've come to watch.'

'And help too,' declared Ana, 'at least, with the little pigs,' she added in her usual quiet voice. 'My grandfather had pigs and they can be quite a handful.'

'Good to see you, Vadek,' said Tadek, shaking his hand.

They all trooped round the side of the house to the yard where the pigs were kept in two separate pens under a corrugated iron roof. Each pen had a small fence with a gate, and there was a walkway from one to the other. The sow had given birth to eleven piglets several weeks previously and now needed to be moved into the bigger pen with her litter.

'That's a big pig,' commented Vadek, as he looked into the pen at the sow lying in the corner, surrounded by her family. 'I hope she's friendly … I've never been that keen on pigs; you can't make friends with a pig like you can a horse or even a cow. Pigs just stare at you, like this one's doing.'

'That's because she likes you,' said Andrzei. 'Just leave everything to me.'

'You obviously know nothing about pigs,' said Henja. 'But you will after today,' and she and Ana collapsed in a fit of giggles.

Andrzei shot an exasperated look at his cousin and raised his eyebrows, rolling his eyes upwards. Vadek grinned.

'Okay, when I open this gate, they'll all run about everywhere,' Tadek said. 'So herd them towards to the other pen as soon as they get out and don't let them go anywhere else.'

'Sounds easy enough to me. You ready?' Andrzei looked at Vadek, who nodded.

'Now!' Tadek shouted, opening the gate. All eleven piglets hurled themselves at the gap. Andrzei, who had positioned himself at the gate rather like a goalkeeper, was taken by surprise and almost bowled over as they rushed between his legs. Squealing, the piglets ran about in every direction except where they were supposed to go. He dived after the last one as it scampered through, but missed its tail and sprawled ungainly on the floor. Annoyed at himself for not managing to grab even one of them, Andrzei stood up and shook the dust and straw from his hair.

'Yes, well, I tripped,' he said to nobody in particular, hoping no-one had noticed. Henja had, but she knew better than to reveal this to Andrzei, whose temper was well known in Kapice.

'I've got one!' shouted Vadek, holding tightly onto a squirming piglet.

'Here!' cried Ana, holding a sack open under the piglet just as it wriggled free. Triumphantly she held it aloft, beaming.

'Humph,' snorted Andrzei. 'You were lucky, that's all.'

Vadek was impressed. 'That was very quick thinking of you.'

Ana smiled as she said graciously, 'We both did it.'

'Only ten more to go,' said Tadek as he took the wriggling sack from Ana and let the animal run free in the new pen; but it was the only occupant.

'They're all back in the pen, but it's the wrong one!' he said.

And so they were, happily back with their mother, who had not moved and was still lying there, unperturbed by the proceedings.

'We need a new tactic,' he said. 'If only we had something to give them they really like.'

'I have!' said Vadek, 'Apples. Two large apples; look!' He lifted up the flaps of his pockets exposing the top of a large apple in each one.

'Now he tells us,' said Andrzei.

'The only problem is, I can't get them out,' said Vadek, struggling to get his fingers round the fruit. 'They're wedged in tight.'

Tadek was gently pushing Vadek towards the pen, who hadn't really noticed, so intent was he on trying to prise an apple from his pocket.

'Don't worry; once she smells them, she'll follow you.'

The sow was now watching Vadek closely. 'I don't like the look of those eyes,' he said warily.

'She's just being friendly, that's all,' said Henja. 'Here, Piggy Piggy, come and get a nice juicy apple.'

'Piggy, Piggy,' said Andrzei, still cross with himself. 'What kind of name is *that*?'

'Erm, that is her name, actually,' said Tadek. 'Henja kept calling her that and it sort of stuck.'

The sow had now risen to her feet and was pushing her huge bulk against Vadek as he stood at the open gate, snuffling her large snout into his jacket but unable to get at the apples.

'Now!' Tadek cried, 'Run! She'll follow you, and so will the piglets!' And with a not too gentle push he propelled Vadek in the direction of the new pen.

Startled, almost stumbling, Vadek sprinted across the barn to the new enclosure with the sow lumbering at his heels. For such a large animal she could certainly move, and she kept so close to Vadek that he almost tripped over her as he practically fell through the gate. The piglets were now no trouble at all and were easily herded into the pen as they followed their mother. Once they were safely in, Vadek closed the gate and leapt out, leaving the mother and babies complaining at the loss of the apples and pushing against the gate.

Tadek shook his head, winking at Henja. 'You've done it now. She's really mad!'

'Definitely. Not a happy pig,' said his sister.

'I know; take off your jacket,' said Andrzei, and yanked it off Vadek's shoulders. Then he dropped it onto the floor and stamped on the bulging pockets with gusto, smashing the apples to a pulp.

'I think you're enjoying that a bit too much,' said Tadek.

'Well, we can't let them go hungry now they've smelt the apples. We'll just shake the pockets over the pen … like this … and everyone's happy!' said Andrzei.

As the pigs gobbled the apples, Vadek retrieved his now grubby jacket from his cousin.

'I'm not sure *I* am,' he grumbled, batting the dust off; then he rubbed a handful of straw in his cousin's hair and ran for it. With a yell, Andrzei raced after him as they shouted their goodbyes to Tadek and Henja.

Together they walked back along the lane. Ana was skipping just in front of them and her plaits swung a little as she moved. Andrzei glanced at Vadek and with a nudge, dared him to pull one of them, fully expecting her to be annoyed. After some hesitation, Vadek reached out and gave one a gentle tug; she spun round, but when she saw it was Vadek, and that he was smiling rather bashfully at her, she smiled back before going on her way with a spring in her step and humming to herself. Vadek looked at Andrzei with a quizzical expression and shrugged his shoulders.

'Girls,' he said. 'Never could understand them.'

Startled, Vadek woke with a jolt as a fellow prisoner he recognised as Thomask, not much older than himself, was shaking him with some urgency: 'Get up! Hurry, there's something happening!'

Vadek climbed down from the bunk, flinching from the pain of his frostbitten feet, and crossed the hut to the open door. Outside, guards were milling about, shouting abrupt orders and the dogs were barking loudly, sensing the urgency of the situation. Army trucks screeched through the open gates and pulled up sharply in the middle of the compound. Men in uniform jumped out, brandishing rifles with fixed bayonets.

Vadek pushed his way through the throng of Polish prisoners now milling around outside, trying to find out what the commotion was all about.

'It's the secret police,' Thomask whispered behind him. 'What can they want?'

Heavy boots crunched as the dreaded NKVD marched across the camp to the furthest barracks. Here the Polish officers were housed separately from the men, as befitting their rank, though their conditions and treatment were no different.

There was silence as, with the other men, Vadek watched the officers being ushered from their huts with their hands behind their heads. Some had clearly not even been given time to dress properly against the freezing temperatures; though it was mid-April it was still bitterly cold and the men had been asleep. Those not moving fast enough were helped along by a rifle butt in the back.

There were murmurs of protest from some of the bewildered men, 'What's going on? It's two in the morning for goodness' sake!'

That earned him a blow in the stomach from a rifle butt. As he doubled up in pain, more voices of dissent could be heard, shouting in protest against the treatment meted out. The prisoners watching, Vadek amongst them, began to shout, demanding to know what was happening to their officers.

Suddenly, there was a burst of machine-gun fire, and they crouched low as bullets rained over their heads, the noise echoing dramatically over the landscape. The police were shouting now, expecting to be obeyed without question. Against so many armed police and guards, there was nothing anyone could do except comply. Helplessly, Vadek and the others watched as the officers were herded like cattle into covered trucks.

'They're going to kill them. They're going to shoot the lot!'

There was stunned silence as the impact of the words sank in. Surely this couldn't be happening. There were codes of conduct even with the enemy. But the Russians were a law unto themselves and answered to no one.

And it was happening. All they could do was watch in horror as the flaps were pulled down and the prisoners could no longer be seen. As the trucks began to move out someone started to sing; a lone voice softly singing a Polish song. More voices joined in, to show solidarity and support, becoming louder, swelling with confidence and pride.

'Poland isn't dead whilst we live. What the foe took by force we will take back with the sword. March, march, Dabrowski, from Italy's soil to Poland! Under your leadership, we will unite the nation.'

All Polish people knew this song; Vadek had sung it as a child and so they sang as with one voice, the words ringing out loud and clear in the night sky until the last of the trucks was swallowed up in the distance. Only then did the voices slowly die, until there was nothing but empty silence in an empty place.

Three months later, on 10 July 1940, an epic battle began over the skies of southern England. Two Polish air force squadrons, 302 and 303, had been formed in England, fighting under the command of the Royal Air Force, but due to language difficulties the Polish contingent joined the fray only in late August. Yet despite its late entry, 303 Squadron claimed the highest number of enemy aircraft shot down in the whole of the Battle of Britain, which ended on 31 October.

SIX

CAMP KOLA, JUNE 1940–JUNE 1941

GERMANY HAVING SEIZED THE PREY, SOVIET RUSSIA WILL SEIZE THAT PART OF THE CARCASS THAT GERMANY CANNOT USE. IT WILL PLAY THE NOBLE ROLE OF HYENA TO THE GERMAN LION.

THE *NEW YORK TIMES* ON THE JOINT INVASION OF POLAND BY GERMANY AND THE SOVIET UNION, 1939

The brutal treatment and punishing regime of the gulag had sapped – as intended – the mental and physical strength of the formerly proud soldiers, and pushed many of them beyond the realms of endurance.

Stalin had refused to sign the Geneva Convention for Polish prisoners of war, and so no Red Cross food parcels were allowed, and no letters could be written or received. No news was permitted from the outside world, and any details of what was happening in the war were concealed, to further weaken morale. This was a labour camp, and the prisoners were there to work for Stalin; this was their only use, and no compassion or mercy was shown to them by their guards.

Each tormented day was the same as the one before. Every day the men slaved for fourteen hours while battling the elements, for even during the short summer months the permafrost made the ground iron hard. The weather was volatile and extreme; one moment the sun could create severe burns, while the next an ice storm would blast across the terrain, mercilessly battering the prisoners.

But even this terrible wilderness could bring new wonders to those who still retained the ability to appreciate them.

Due to the proximity to the North Pole, in summer the days and nights became as one; with the sun never setting between May and July it was daylight for twenty-four hours of every day. In winter the opposite was true; then the deep turquoise haze of twilight would last just a few brief hours before darkness descended, enveloping the endless wilderness in a blanket pierced by millions of stars scattered across the vast Arctic sky, and the brilliance of the moon as she progressed regularly through her phases.

In contrast, the unpredictability of the dancing display of Northern Lights lent an edge to their multi-coloured hues, in vivid contrast to the snow. Vadek felt humbled in their presence, for it was impossible for him not to be mesmerised by the performance. Caused by energetic particles from solar storms colliding with the earth's atmosphere, the lights can turn the sky around the magnetic poles into a vast glowing work of kinetic art, and with thoughts never far from home, Vadek knew that his little brother would have been held spellbound by them. How ironic, he thought, that the most spectacular natural phenomenon he had ever witnessed was in the most hostile of environments he had ever encountered.

Always mind-numbingly cold and ravenously hungry, the prisoners were unable to revive their flagging spirits. Breakfast was a mug of weak black tea with a chunk of dry rye bread, though this 'bread' was a mix of flour with sawdust added. But starving men do not notice or care about such things. Tea was a fish soup of boiled water with a few herrings thrown in, often containing nothing more than a fish head or bone.

The soup was cooked outdoors in huge pans that resembled saucepans, as each had a long handle enabling the cook to hold it over an open fire without getting too close to the flames. But as this was the only time there was any heat, the men tried to get as near to the fire as they could. Then, with only a few minutes to get bowls filled, there was much jostling and pushing in the queue, for there might be nothing left at all left for the last in line. Greedily, they gulped the soup while standing outside or sitting in the snow. No talking was permitted at any time. Occasionally, a bowl would be knocked from a hand by a passing guard, who would laugh as the prisoner scrabbled in the snow for any dregs. But even worse, a guard might occasionally tip the whole saucepan over, apparently enjoying the shock and horror on the faces of the starving prisoners.

Here there was no longer any pride in one's regiment; only desperation driven by relentless hunger knowing that without any nourishment, however meagre, your body could not possibly survive.

With barely time to finish their food, the men were marched two abreast several miles into the wilderness; the walk felt twice as long because of the constant battle with the elements. Here they were put to work assembling runways and clearing the ground in readiness for use by Russian military aircraft. This meant felling the trees and digging the stumps out of the frozen ground; a back-breaking task for fit men, let alone ones so undernourished and weak. It would take many days before an area was flat enough for the metal access tracks to be laid, that task too made infinitely more difficult by the permafrost.

The icy wind was like a razor blade cutting into the very marrow of the bone. It never failed to penetrate the prisoners' worn, frayed clothes. Hands, numb in thin, tattered gloves, were unable to hold the tools to position the iron nuts and bolts. These would then drop from stiff fingers, resulting in a feverish scramble to pick them up before being beaten senseless. Feet went black with frostbite in split, worn boots, while eyebrows, hair, even eyelashes, turned white in the frosty air. The ice could seal eyelids shut and stick frozen fingers to metal. Bones and joints became as fragile as glass, so they could break with the slightest pressure, yet no pain would be felt; then they would reset themselves awkwardly without a person even knowing. Until much later.

A man could be clubbed to death for whispering to his neighbour. Except for the taunts and abuse from the guards, the long, gruelling day would pass in silence.

At the end of it, the exhausted men trudged the miles back to the barracks, feet dragging, with stabbing pain at every step. Bodies hunched and heads bent, battling against a wind so fierce it took a supreme effort of will to keep upright and force one foot in front of the other in the snow, which hampered movement and sapped any strength that was left. Visibility was often reduced, with flurries of snow like shards of glass battering haggard faces and stinging the eyes.

The guards would taunt the prisoners, encouraging them to escape: 'Go on, we won't stop you,' they would jeer. 'Make a run for it, why don't you?'

Then they would make a big show of laying their guns on the ground and waving their arms above their heads. 'Look, we won't shoot you. Go on, run!' And they would laugh at the prisoners' predicament, knowing full well that no-one alone in the wilderness could survive a Siberian winter, with temperatures as low as –50°C (–58°F).

The Russians cared little for the Poles, and one dead Pole was one less to bother about. The tempo set by Stalin was murderous. If a man fell, no help could be given him under threat of immediate death, so he would lie there, too weak to move, until a layer of snow became his coffin.

The guards would then frantically, desperately, pull the coat off the still-warm body before the corpse became stiff and frozen. This sickened Vadek to the very depths of his being and he would turn away in revulsion. Yet he also condoned their behaviour; in a way he understood it. Their situation was little better than that of the prisoners they guarded, and in such barbaric conditions who knew what might happen if the situation was reversed. To stay warm, to stay alive, to survive from one terrible day to the next, men could and did lose all moral sensibilities.

Back at the barracks at the end of each day, the men collapsed onto their bunks. Rarely did anyone speak, but fell immediately into the deep sleep of exhaustion. They slept with their clothes on, partly for extra warmth, though often too tired to make the effort to remove them. Stiff, frozen fingers struggled to untie the stiff, frozen laces of heavy boots, and wrenching frozen feet free of them caused intense pain. But Vadek knew that to keep his blood from freezing he had to remove the boots and massage his toes. All of the men suffered terribly from frostbite, their fingers and toes going black, but many dared not pull their boots off for fear of pulling their toes off with them.

There was no hot water for the prisoners, nor indeed even any cold water, just snow. Many became ill with pneumonia but were forced to work until they dropped, for there was no medical aid, nor any medical supplies of any kind. Without a doctor to treat the frostbite or tend the sick, many inmates simply died in their beds.

At night, alone with his thoughts, the sheer hopelessness of the situation overwhelmed Vadek and he would be consumed with such a tremendous sense of loss and self-pity that it was an extreme effort to pull himself out of the deep abyss of despair. The life he'd had before … it all seemed so long ago and far away; like a dream. The cosy kitchen at home with the smell of bread fresh from the oven; the sun warming his back as he worked in the fields; simple everyday things he had taken for granted – these he now remembered with a deep and heartfelt longing.

Peaceful, tranquil Kapice. Not even a village really, just several farmhouses clustered together with a few more houses dotted about. Sometimes he had craved more excitement, more adventure, for life on the farm could be mundane. A lump came into his throat as he remembered how his life had so drastically changed. All he wanted now was for everything to be as it was before. To return to that slow but secure life with its normality, its simplicity and the pleasures all too easily taken for granted until snatched away in a heartbeat. He felt he would never take anything for granted again.

He tried to remember a time when he hadn't been cold. Was there such a time? He could barely remember. Would he ever feel warm again? Was there even such a thing? It was such a distant memory. Now it was so cold that the brain became numb, the body refused to move and every muscle had to be forced to work by a superhuman effort of will. It would be so easy to give up. Let the cold take over and sleep …

Then there was the relentless hunger; the never-ending gnawing deep in the pit of the stomach like a knot being pulled ever tighter. Every minute of every hour of every day. What did real food taste like? He had forgotten.

And the thirst … always so incredibly thirsty. He had resorted to eating the snow. However, he knew better than to gulp it, for too much would freeze his mouth and throat, burning his tongue, while the energy needed from his body to thaw it meant he would be losing valuable heat. So he placed very small pieces on his tongue and waited for each one to melt before swallowing. He did this frequently, every day, always with the smallest amounts. Or sometimes he would crush it between his numb hands then lick the droplets from his fingers. Consumption of snow was the only way to prevent himself dehydrating completely.

He tried not to think what might happen if Poland lost the war. What would become of them, of everyone? There would be no life. There was no doubt in his mind, all Poles would be better off dead.

Wanting to extinguish those thoughts before they became too much to bear, Vadek tried to blot them out by thinking of his home and the family, waiting for him.

And of course there was Ana. Strange, he thought, how it was possible not to notice someone simply because they were always there. In the background: at school, in church and even on the farm. Ruefully he remembered the little smiles she had given him, which he had mostly ignored. Well, like most teenage boys, he hadn't really been much interested in girls back then, seeing them as more of a nuisance.

Of course there had been a few girls at university, but none had held his interest for long, maybe because deep down he was missing Ana and didn't even know it. Love was a funny thing, he decided, pulling his blanket around him as closely as he could, in a vain attempt to instil some warmth into his body. A smile lit up his eyes. Yes; he resolved that as soon as he could, he would write her a letter telling her how he felt. After all, the war couldn't last for ever. As his eyes closed and sleep washed over him, he was composing it.

SEVEN

CAMP KOLA, JUNE 1941

**IMPOSING COMMUNISM ON CATHOLIC POLAND IS AS
ABSURD AS PUTTING A SADDLE ON A COW.**

JOSEF STALIN

It was early in the morning, maybe about 4 am, and Vadek awoke, needing to go to the latrines. The light from outside filtered in through the frosted coating of the window; Vadek could never get used to the days that had no nights. Leaving his bunk, he quietly moved past the sleeping men and went outside, for the door was never locked. Where could they run to? There was nothing out there for over a thousand miles, and only a fool or a madman would attempt to escape. Vadek was neither. The only chance of survival was in the camp.

He trod as silently as he could manage, for he did not want to attract any attention. But the snow crunched underfoot as he rounded the side of the hut and made his way to the outer perimeter where the latrines were. They were nothing more than wells dug into the snow with a channel running between each one. The searchlights could not quite reach them.

As quickly as he could he finished his business and blew through his fingers, trying to instil some warmth into them, but his breath too was cold and sharp. Vadek often felt claustrophobic in the hut, for he was used to being outside, in open farmland. He sighed. Would he ever see his home again?

Standing there, with some difficulty, he reached his gloved hand into the inside pocket of his coat, stiff fingers fumbling as he pulled out a badly creased photograph. He looked at it tenderly, his eyes misting over. There was his mother holding his new little baby brother, Stanislav, who he barely knew. There was his father, with his arm proudly and protectively round them both, with Roman sitting on his shoulders, waving madly. Vadek wistfully ran his finger across the photo. Surely every soldier carried a photo of his loved ones in his pocket, he thought with a wry smile. He hoped fervently that the war hadn't been unkind to his family.

'Who goes there?' The command jolted him out of his reverie and startled, he dropped the photo which fluttered to the ground. Vadek looked up – straight into the end of a rifle.

He froze. The sentry held his rifle unsteadily in trembling hands, and his voice faltered as he asked sternly, 'What are you doing?'

'Nothing.' Vadek replied quietly in Russian, slowly lifting his eyes and fixing them on the man at the other end of the rifle, who now held his life in his hands. He couldn't have been much older than Vadek – maybe even younger; it was difficult to tell these days as the ravages of war affected them all.

Vadek pointed to the photograph, now on the ground by his boot. The sentry dropped his gaze but not his rifle. Seeing the photograph lying there, he gestured to Vadek to pick it up. Very slowly, Vadek bent and groped for the photograph, his eyes never leaving the sentry's face. He straightened up and held it towards him. The sentry slowly took it from his outstretched hand and stared at it for a moment. As he handed the photo back, his face softened. '*Rodzina?*' he asked simply.

'Yes, my family,' Vadek replied in quiet tones, his breath frosty in the cold still air.

Lowering his rifle, the sentry was now reaching into the breast pocket of his army greatcoat where he pulled out a photograph. Badly creased and lined many times over, it had obviously been removed and folded again and again. He pushed it into Vadek's hand, his face now lighting up as he said, '**Moj** *rodzina!*' and repeated it twice as he pointed with his finger to the people grouped together in the photograph.

Relieved that the rifle was no longer pointing at him, Vadek breathed more easily. He looked silently at the picture in his hand and saw a family not unlike his own: a man and a woman standing together, holding the hands of a pretty blonde girl of about five, and next to them in a Russian army uniform, the young sentry in front of him. As Vadek gazed at the smiling group taken in happier times, he felt a strange sense of comradeship for the Russian soldier. He was just like him. Torn away from his loved ones to fight in a war he hadn't chosen to be part of. In fact he looked like he was in need of a good meal too.

They gazed at each other for a minute in silence, and as Vadek looked into the face of his enemy – a person he should hate but somehow didn't – he saw a sadness in his eyes and felt a sense of kindred spirit. This young man was not a member of the NKVD, the dreaded Russian secret police; he was a young soldier on guard duty just doing his job in the same hellhole as the prisoners and undergoing the same horrendous conditions.

'Marek.' The soldier volunteered his name, and the thought struck Vadek that the soldier was probably just as homesick as he was.

'Vadek,' he said just as simply. Marek nodded, and for a minute they just stood there. Two young men, caught up in a war neither wanted, both wanting to go home and leave this hostile land, and doing what they had to do to survive.

Suddenly Marek grabbed his photograph and shoved it back into his pocket, then turning quickly he disappeared round the back of the hut. Shaken, Vadek stayed stock still. He could hear the crunch of heavy boots coming nearer, and held his breath. It would have done neither of them any good to be caught talking to each other, for they were enemies and could both be shot.

'Something the matter?' came brusque tones from around the corner.

'Nothing, nothing,' stammered Marek. 'Just taking a pee.'

The other sentry said. 'Is that all? Well, better be quick then, before it falls off in this godforsaken place,' and laughed. Their voices faded.

With a sigh of relief, Vadek waited until he could no longer hear their voices, then quickly he slipped back to the safety of the hut. If circumstances had been different, they could have been friends. But in the grim reality of war, friends could not be chosen easily. Like it or not, they were enemies.

EIGHT

CAMP KOLA, JULY 1941

TRUE SOLIDARITY IS FOUND IN A CEMETERY.

JOSEF STALIN

As Vadek lay on his bed, he could not help but listen to the sounds of those around him. Some were restless, repeatedly turning over and muttering in their sleep, while others shouted, reliving memories they would rather forget. Vadek pondered the futility of it all and tried to steer his mind onto another train of thought, remembering when a famous general who had fought in the First World War had paid a visit to his school at Suwalki. This was a great honour and had been the talking point for many weeks.

In the central courtyard all the students had been formed into rigid rows. Andrzei had been barely able to contain his excitement and stand to attention as the general had marched along as if inspecting the troops; he was resplendent in his uniform and his many medals glinted as they caught the summer sunshine.

Andrzei had listened enthralled to the stories the general had related, and was unable to talk of anything else for several days. That same evening, when lounging on the lawn during their permitted talking time, Andrzei was unable to contain himself any longer. He suddenly jumped up, startling Vadek who was sprawled on the grass, hands under head, contemplating the herringbone sky.

'That's what I want to do!' proclaimed Andrzei.

'Do what?' enquired Vadek, wrinkling his brow as he squinted up at his cousin.

'Sit grandly astride my noble steed, charging fearlessly into the fray with my sabre held high!' exclaimed Andrzei. 'Everyone will remember me with

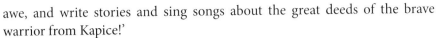

awe, and write stories and sing songs about the great deeds of the brave warrior from Kapice!'

And so saying he proceeded to prance around Vadek, still lying on the ground but wishing he wasn't as he tried to roll over to dodge the swift thrusts of Andrzei's imaginary sword.

'But you can't even ride a horse,' said Vadek.

'Yes, I can!' retorted Andrzei indignantly, not still for a moment and with another sharp dig in Vadek's ribs.

'What! Our old farm horse!' snorted Vadek, brushing the grass from his uniform as he stood up. 'Even my old *babcia* can sit on her without falling off!' They relished the picture he conjured up of Vadek's grandmother galloping around the village and laughed out loud.

'SSShhh…!' The shushing noise came from one of the professors who was strolling through the gardens nearby. With a warning look, he pressed his finger to his lips to emphasise the Sssshh before continuing on his way.

'Okay, Okay,' muttered Andrzei, 'but one day you'll see.' And with that he waltzed off towards the dormitories, with a spring in his step and an occasional thrust of an arm.

Back to reality. Vadek turned over with a sigh, pulling the blanket up to his nose and curling up into a foetal position. Would it ever end? All he wanted to do was go home. To see his family again, his friends, Tadek, Henja … and Ana. To return to university to finish his studies and become a professor of mathematics. He remembered as clearly as if it were only yesterday, the fateful day it had all begun; it all seemed so far away.

By June 1939, he had been studying mathematics at university for a year. He had decided to become a teacher and leave the running of the farm to his father and eventually Roman. Czeslav had been disappointed at first, as their farm was traditionally passed to the eldest son, but he also knew that Vadek's quick mind needed more stimulation than could be provided by the running of a small farm, and he had been very proud when Vadek had been accepted by the prestigious Warsaw University.

Vadek now had another brother, Stanislav, just a few months old. He was healthy and round-faced, and his gurgling would make Roman laugh. Vadek was looking forward to seeing his family and friends in a few weeks when university finished for the summer break.

The last time they had all been together had been the previous Christmas, when snow had lain thick on the ground. They had taken the sleigh out of the barn, and the bells on the harness jingled as it sped along to Midnight Mass. Vadek and Andrzei, wrapped up warmly, chatted non-stop, their breath hanging in the frosty air; their route was lined by fir trees standing majestically, like tall sentinels, beneath the splendour of their winter dress. It was a beautiful night. The stars were as jewels against the velvet sky, and the full moon hung like a huge opalescent globe, bathing everything in its silver-white glow, and illuminating the little church with its snowy mantle.

Inside, all the pews were full and there was little standing room, but Vadek spied Ana with her family, and her face lit up when she saw him. While singing hymns and listening to the service, she continued to give shy, side-long glances at Vadek, who had begun to notice how pretty she was in her red fur hat and matching muff.

Now the ice on the river was solid enough for skating. Sleds were unearthed to take the younger children to the river, shouting at their brothers or sisters to pull them faster despite the eye-watering, cheek-pinching air.

The bank was lined with crowds of children and parents, and Ana with Henja waited for the races to start, spurring their friends on with loud shouts and boisterous yelling. The tall riverbank grasses, crunching underfoot, glinted in the weak winter sunshine.

Several years ago, Vadek's father had made a pair of wooden skates for him. Now Vadek attached them to his boots. Sharpened to a fine edge, the skates cut keenly into the ice as, with hands behind backs and exhilarated faces pushing into the wind, he and the other local boys each strived to be the first to reach the winning post.

Wrapped up against the bitter cold and oblivious to it, face flushed and eyes sparkling, Ana shouted encouragement to Vadek, clapping her hands and jumping up and down. Vadek told himself he wasn't trying to impress her with his prowess – but he stole a glance her way nonetheless, and a surge of happiness spurred him on when he saw she was looking at him.

In the late afternoons, in the quiet of dusk, a fiddler would come and play, and lanterns would add a romantic glow. Then Czeslav and Camilla would join the dancing, swirling around elegantly on the ice in their coats and hats, gaining just as great an enjoyment from their more sedate activity as the energetic racers earlier.

But these were times of political upheaval and a cloud loomed over the festivities and the banter. Talk had turned to the unrest that had been settling over Europe, for their south-westerly neighbour, Czechoslovakia, had been crushed by Hitler and his army earlier that year. Polish intelligence had had the foresight, even before this ominous incident, to give a German enigma machine to the British, after breaking the code.

As early as 1933, Hitler had confided to his generals his plans for expansion: first to recover the Sudetenland – the German area of Czechoslovakia, partitioned after the First World War – second to annex Austria, and third to take France, Russia and Poland.

There had already been continuing disputes over Poland's busiest port, Danzig on the Baltic coast, which had been a German city before partition, and to this were added the unsettling news reports of anti-Semitism that had been filtering through during the past year. Reports of Polish Jews living in Germany being left stranded on the borders. Reports of the Kristallnacht, the Night of Broken Glass, in November 1938, when the shops and business premises of thousands of Jews all over Germany were destroyed.

So the winter days of 1938–39 were disturbing times, and with the unstable relationship with the Russians on the eastern side, it was clear that Poland would be sandwiched between two aggressors. Every evening, people would gather around the radio and listen anxiously for further developments. However life had to go on, and it was against this background of uncertainty that Vadek returned to university after New Year, trying, as they all did, to quell any fears about the future; for Hitler was in Germany, and surely what happened there could not affect Poland. There were more pressing things to be concerned about; after all he had exams to pass …

Late August, and as usual the holidays had gone by all too quickly with so much catching up to do with friends, and of course getting to know his new brother. Stanislav was always crawling into everything. Roman was now an eleven-year-old budding farmer, following his father everywhere, demanding to know about everything.

Ana had become a frequent visitor to the Kossakowski home, often staying for Sunday lunch and helping Camilla prepare the meal. Afterwards if the weather was fine she and Vadek would take a quiet stroll together or take the horse and cart for a jaunt.

It was the first day of September, and the next day Vadek would be returning to university. His mother had prepared a special dinner for the occasion with *bigos* and of course *pączki* – still a firm favourite with Vadek, who now found he had a rival when he saw Roman stuffing them into his already full mouth.

'Who does that remind you of?' said his father as he poured out a measure of vodka to celebrate Vadek's success at university.

The radio was on playing music softly so as not to wake the baby. The clear liquid tinkled into the glasses and through the half-open doorway the late evening sunshine caught the drops, forming minuscule rainbows. Roman was fascinated.

A voice interrupted the music; the president, Ignacy Mościcki, was speaking. Camilla turned up the volume, sternly shushing Roman. They listened, then sat in stunned silence, hardly daring to breathe in case they missed something, listening but not quite comprehending. Surely there was a misunderstanding. It could not be true.

Germany had invaded Poland!

Camilla's glass dropped from her hand into shards of glass and a small pool of vodka. She held her hands to her ashen face, shaking her head: 'No,' she whispered, '*It can't be true.*'

Stanislav, sensing that something was wrong, climbed onto his mother's lap, whimpering, pulling at her hands, wanting a cuddle. The family sat in stunned silence, Vadek's hands on the table, his fingers clenched around his glass, Czeslav's face set as if in stone.

They were startled by a hammering on the door, and Andrzei's brother Pavel burst through, his tall frame blocking the last rays of sun as it sank below the horizon.

'Have you heard …?' he began, then stopped as he realised they had.

'Yes, we heard,' Czeslav replied in hushed tones. 'We heard.'

Pavel stood there. A moment in time that would be imprinted on the memory for ever.

Motionless, they listened to more of the broadcast. All young men were being asked to report immediately at the nearest army recruitment centre. They looked at each other. For Vadek there would be no more lazy summers. His mother fell to her knees and wept.

But in fact war had been inevitable, for Adolf Hitler had been stirring up tension in Germany for several months and was prepared to fabricate whatever was needed as a pretext to invade Poland, informing the League of Nations High Commissioner that: 'If there's the slightest provocation, I shall shatter Poland without warning into so many pieces there will be nothing left.'

And to his military commanders on 22 August: 'I will give cause for war whether convincing or not. The winner is not asked whether he told the truth or not.'

To that end Hitler instigated several skirmishes along the border, including a 'false flag' incident at Gleiwitz on 31 August. On that fateful evening, German operatives dressed in Polish uniforms seized the radio station and, speaking in Polish, called for all Poles to take up arms against Germany.

As with the Sudetenland and Austria, Hitler never officially declared war on Poland; he just invented an excuse to invade, and did so on 1 September 1939. But this time, the moves were overtly aggressive: the massive German battleship *Schleswig-Holstein* shelled Danzig, and the Luftwaffe bombed Warsaw and the market towns of Wielun and Frampol, in the pre-planned Operation Wasserkante.

And so began the Second World War.

NINE

CAMP KOLA, JULY 1941

SOLDIER, LOST IN SIBERIAN WINTERS, DEVASTATED BY
SCURVY, RAVAGED BY DECAY, OUT OF THIS SHAME AND
FILTH, DISGRACE AND PUTRID WASTE, TO SERVE THE
COUNTRY GAVE YOU ANOTHER CHANCE.

FELIKS KONARSKI, POW

The intolerable conditions in the camp combined with the extreme weather and inhuman treatment had taken their toll, and Vadek had become a walking skeleton of rags and lice. His coat hung loose while his boots had almost disintegrated, held together only by frozen laces. A shadow of his former self, the hollow eyes and pinched cheekbones in his famished face gave him the appearance of a man very much older. Most of his teeth had fallen out due to the poor diet, and he suffered badly from frostbite; but in that at least he was one of the lucky ones as many had lost their toes or fingers, even both.

The once amazing spectacle of the Northern Lights had long ago ceased to enthral him, and now paled into insignificance as he struggled to live long enough to get through this terrible experience. The fear that he would die here in this hell on earth, and never see a loved one again was often too much to bear and in his worse moments he feared for his sanity.

The daily mental and physical abuse from the guards became a terrifying ordeal of fearful apprehension, for an opportunity was never missed to ridicule and humiliate the prisoners. Often in the most horrific way. Purely for sadistic amusement, or from sheer boredom, or merely from his eye being caught, a guard could knock a prisoner to the ground, beat him senseless or shoot him. From one day to the next, no prisoner knew if he was going to be singled out, nor which day would be his last. The constant cramps of hunger, the extreme physical exertion and the ever-present fear of death strained the former soldiers to the limits of their endurance, and the pressure on them to keep a grip on reason was immeasurable.

In spring 1941, events in north Africa had prompted the Italian leader Benito Mussolini to ask Hitler for assistance; he responded promptly by sending the crack German Afrika Korps, under the brilliant General Erwin Rommel. The city of Tobruk was vital to the operations in north Africa, and the siege was to last eight months. During that summer, the Polish Independent Carpathian Rifle Brigade was deployed to help the Australians in north Africa. The brigade was formed of exiled Polish soldiers who had evaded capture when Poland was invaded by Germany and who had made their way to France and other Allied countries. Such was their impact during the siege of Tobruk that the Australians nicknamed them the Tobruk Rats.

That same summer, fate was to intervene in the life of Vadek and the other prisoners of war in Camp Kola. On 22 June, Germany and its allies had launched Operation Barbarossa, a massive invasion of the Soviet Union on a 1000-mile (1500-km) front running from the Baltic to the Black Sea.

Hitler had set his sights on the oilfields of the Russian Caucasus, but his real objective was the Baku oilfields in Azerbaijan by the Caspian Sea, once part of Persia (Iran) but which now belonged to Stalin's Russia. Without warning, Hitler broke the Treaty of Non-Aggression which he and Stalin had signed in the August of 1939.

Stalin was taken by surprise, for though he had harboured some distrust of the German leader, he implicitly believed that Hitler would want to defeat Britain before trying anything else. Rashly – with hindsight – he had chosen to ignore the information to the contrary that he received from his spies in Germany, and he now was left with no option but to ally himself with the British – and the Poles.

When the Germans invaded the Russian western military districts and wrecked much of their wire network, such was the confusion that transmissions such as this:

We are being fired upon. What shall we do?

were responded to thus:

You must be insane! And why is your signal not in code?

Unbeknownst to Stalin, some years earlier Hitler had in fact declared his intention to invade the Soviet Union to the League of Nations commissioner, Carl Jacob Burckhardt. On 11 August 1939 – just a few days before signing the Non-Aggression Pact with Stalin – Hitler had told Burckhardt: 'Everything I undertake is directed at the Russians. If the West is too stupid and blind to grasp this, then I shall be compelled to come to an agreement with the Russians, beat the West, then after their defeat turn against the Soviets with all my forces. I need the Ukraine so they cannot starve us out as they did in the last war.'

Early morning, and soldiers came bursting into the huts, shouting for everyone to go outside. The whole camp was in a state of turmoil, soldiers darting about, unsure what to do. In the central compound the commandant was barking orders. Then, flanked by armed guards, he faced the assembled prisoners and addressed them loudly in Polish: By order of the Great Russian Leader Josef Stalin, they were being released to fight with the Russians and their allies against Germany. They were being liberated!

There was a moment of shock, disbelief. No one could find a voice. Liberated? They were free? Realisation began to dawn, and with it, loud murmurs of protest from the incredulous Poles.

Standing next to Vadek, his friend Thomask loudly voiced his discontent, as did several others. Remembering the massacred officers, he said: 'Not me; there's no way I'll fight for that murderer!'

Vadek remained silent and wished fervently that Thomask had not spoken out so rashly, for he knew this was their way out. The only way out. They had been given a lifeline. An event had occurred which no one in the camp could possibly have imagined. Hitler had turned on his erstwhile ally. On that fateful day, the course of Vadek's life changed.

The commandant snapped his fingers and a guard ran forward to stand directly in front of Thomask, who stood his ground, yet was unsure of what was going to happen next. In one rapid movement the guard pointed his gun directly at Thomask's head, his finger on the trigger.

'If you do not fight for the Russians you will die, for you are of no use to our Great and Glorious Leader, Josef Stalin.'

A flash. A shot rang out. The noise was deafening. A smell of cordite. Thomask's head jerked back, his body convulsed, and slipped sideways. He fell to the ground. No one moved. There was stunned silence. It had happened so quickly, it was almost as if it hadn't happened at all.

Vadek stared straight ahead, his eyes full of the horror he had just witnessed. Blood splattered his cheek. His face. He tried to control his trembling. But he could not. The stench of blood filled his nostrils. His friend, his compatriot, was dead. And the pure white of the snow became stained with the bright red of fresh blood.

The Poles and Russians having been bitter enemies for centuries, the Soviet leader would not allow the now-freed Polish prisoners of war to carry arms – and they in turn were loath to fight alongside the Russians, who they did not trust. But a desperate Stalin was forced to look for allies. And so, under the Sikorksi–Mayski agreement of 30 July, followed by an amendment signed on 14 August, the former Polish prisoners were given an amnesty to form an army, to be led by Polish officers – but under Soviet command. However, there were many obstacles to be overcome, with multiple differences and disputes. For example, according to Soviet data, only 21,000 Polish troops had been imprisoned, and 1,000 officers, but the Polish government knew that there were many thousands more; many thousands of Polish soldiers were only released from detention in Russia after emphatic intervention by the Polish embassy and army headquarters.

The demanding task of forming the army began three days later, in the small Russian town of Totskoye, one of two army replacement camps; the other was at Tatiszczewo, Saratova. It fell to General Sikorski, the head of the Polish government in exile in London, and commander in chief of the Polish armed forces, to choose the new army's commander.

The Polish general Władysław Anders had served in the Russian army during the First World War, and then against the Russians in the Polish–Soviet war of 1919–21. A cavalry officer at the outset of the Second World War, he was captured and imprisoned by the Russians – but luckily he was known to Sikorski, who offered him the position of commander under the amnesty for Polish prisoners. Near death from torture, Anders was released from Moscow's Lubyanka Prison on 4 August 1941, and announced his appointment eighteen days later.

Vadek, with his fellow prisoners, was liberated from Camp Kola on 27 July, five days after Germany had invaded the Soviet Union. But no one knew what was happening or where they would go. The Russians had decamped, taking all available modes of transport, and the ex-prisoners were left alone in the frozen wilderness. Hundreds of miles from any type of civilisation, all they could do was wait. In terrible suspense.

A few days later, liaison officers from Polish army headquarters arrived to escort the ex-prisoners on a journey of almost a thousand miles; to the internment camp in Suzdal. The exhausted men were then confined in what had originally been a monastery, had been used as a forbidding Russian prison, and was now an effective holding cell. Stark and unwelcoming, it was here that they stayed until 25 August, when a traumatised Vadek endured another gruelling five-hundred-mile journey before he at last arrived at the army placement camp at Tatiszczewo.

A few days later, on 4 September, Vadek officially became part of the new Fifth Infantry Division of the Polish Army, under the command of General Anders.

Vadek was one of the lucky ones; many had not survived the journey. After so long in captivity and suffering from such terrible conditions, many of the former prisoners were dead on arrival. How Vadek had survived that journey when so many had not he did not know. He had sat there, in that cold, cramped truck, motionless, expressionless, still in shock after seeing his friend murdered in front of his eyes. Sometimes, still feeling the blood spattering his face, he would raise a hand to wipe it. So close to freedom. So close. To suffer those years in the camp, and for what? To die. To *die on the very day you were freed*. He could not bear it. But he could not shut it out. And there around him, sharing his truck, were more dead bodies. On that nightmare journey, all he could see was the bloody face of his friend. But worse was to come.

Life at the replacement camp was truly horrific; incredibly overcrowded with so little room in the tents that many of the new arrivals had to sleep outdoors, while the food was little different from that of the prison camp. The fish soup was cooked in huge pans over camp fires in the snow by the men themselves after first chopping the firewood. Often so cold and weak, it took then a supreme effort of will to do this. The unbearable cold made reflexes slow, and the mind seemed to shut down, making it difficult to concentrate. With the exception of the brutality so frequently inflicted on them by their former captors, the conditions were not dissimilar to what they had previously endured.

The agonies of another Russian winter were forced upon them with even the November temperatures in the steppes falling below −20°C (−4°F). As a consequence, the camp commandant was forced to order the men to go out in relays to chop wood to build dug-outs in the snow. For those who were left with no option but to sleep outside, there was the nightmare of not knowing if they would survive the night, and their worst fears were often proved correct.

Vadek dreaded going to sleep. Due to being one of the first arrivals he was fortunate to be able to sleep in the tent – but with no bed, mattress or even a blanket, he resorted to using the branches and foliage from the pines to give him some protection from the icy ground. However, with so little comfort and warmth he knew he might not wake and that each night could be his last. Routinely he would press his cold lips to the faded photo of his family and utter a quiet prayer. More often than not it was this fear, coupled with the intense cold, that kept him awake. The repeated trauma of waking next to a body, someone who perhaps had been a friend, was something he could never erase completely from his mind in later years. And worse, having to drag the frozen body from the tent to be buried in a makeshift grave was so deeply disturbing that he felt he could not bear to go through another day, another night.

Nights which were full of awful, terrible dreams, when he saw dead people. Murdered comrades in front of his eyes, reaching out to him, closer, closer … then he would wake screaming, shaking, shouting in fear, so horrified that he did not want to close his eyes again lest they reach him … and he would pray for the sweet kiss of death. The release and peace that only death could bring. And he would be free.

That winter the course of the war was to alter dramatically, when without warning Japan attacked the US naval base at Pearl Harbor, Hawaii, on 7 December just before 8 am. President Franklin Delano Roosevelt declared war on Japan the next day; Germany and Italy sided with Japan, and they in turn declared war on the United States a few days later, on 11 December 1941.

The Red Army wanted all the Poles transferred to the Eastern Front as soon as possible despite their pitiful condition. The aim, to resist the German advance towards the oil fields of the Caucasus, primarily Baku. Both sides needed oil for their armoured divisions. But General Anders refused to transfer his men on the grounds that they were not sufficiently recovered nor even prepared, having had no proper training and having no arms or equipment. They were desperately in need of boots and were still wearing their prison camp rags. In retaliation, Stalin, who had no regard whatsoever for the Poles' welfare or well-being, cut the supply rate.

The Soviet authorities had been unwilling to give up their prisoners as they wanted the slave labour, and the Russian government resented the idea of supplying their former enemies with food. This was another reason for essential supplies such as clothes and food being reduced. Meat, fats and vegetables were completely absent from the food supply, and the bread quota was cut yet again, causing extreme distress to the already starving men and becoming a cause of great concern for General Anders.

The former prisoners stayed at the camp in southern Russia until the end of December, when they were permitted to relocate to the more southern Soviet Asian republics – Kazakhstan, Uzbekistan and Turkmenistan – departing in the second week of January, 1942. The journey would take four weeks, and many died in the crowded convoy trucks, too weak to survive such an arduous trip.

With troops still suffering from malnutrition and barely enough food to support them all, General Anders wrote to the Polish commander in chief: 'The men are starving; already many are suffering from night blindness. There is no hope of improvement, quite the opposite, the situation continues to deteriorate and the only hope lies in leaving the Soviet Union.'

But before the Polish units had arrived at their new locations, there was a change of plan. Due to political reasons the Soviet Union withdrew its limited support for the Polish army on Russian territory, and after new negotiations between the Soviet leader and Winston Churchill, it was decided to send the Poles to Iran and from there to Iraq to reinforce the British Eighth Army in the Middle East. Here they would be under the command of the British, and four new divisions would be formed, based on the British system.

The journey across Russia in large covered army trucks took several weeks and covered over two thousand miles. Vadek was leaving Russia, and this action undoubtedly saved his, and many other lives, for under Russian control he surely would have perished.

For the first time in two years, despite the trauma of the events surrounding him, Vadek felt a lifting of his spirits and a surge of hope. He was at last able to wonder what the future might bring. There was a new enthusiasm in his mind and body which was reflected in his eyes; perhaps now he could dare hope that maybe one day, not only he but all of Poland would be free. He was no longer waiting to die.

Tarpaulin covers provided protection from the weather as the convoy bumped over the uneven ground for mile after mile. Progress was painfully slow due to blown bridges and fallen trees. Ironically, this could have been caused by either the enemy or the Polish resistance; weeks were spent rebuilding the bridges and clearing the roads.

Everywhere Russia was on the move, crowded with refugees fleeing bombed-out cities in the face of the Germans' relentless advance. Hundreds of people were on the march; carts piled high with belongings or people simply carrying what they could on their backs, children with no shoes, crying for lost mothers. The sick and the elderly had no choice but to leave their homes, and were all on the move or dying where they lay, too weak or ill to go any further.

Vadek felt some sympathy for these people who had lost their homes and their families – everything they owned – and his thoughts would turn often to his own family. What was happening in Bialystok? In Kapice? In Warsaw? He had tried desperately to find any news of Andrzei, but it had been impossible and he could only hope and pray that he would see him again one day.

Constantly on the move, always one step ahead of the enemy, or sometimes one step behind, the convoy reached bombed-out towns with nothing left but starving people, scrabbling in the ruins of their destroyed homes for whatever they could salvage.

IRAQ AND PALESTINE, 1942

In late spring of 1942, the convoy finally reached the Caspian Sea. Here, Vadek left his homeland far behind him for the final leg of the journey in boats and trucks to the heat and dust of Iran, then Iraq. He was not to know that he would not see his homeland again for over twenty-five years.

In north Africa, the July sun scorched the deserts from dawn till dusk. On the northern coast of Egypt, the battle for El Alamein, under the German command of Field Marshal Rommel, the Desert Fox, was under way. But in mid-August the tide would turn in favour of the Allies, when General Bernard Montgomery assumed command of the British forces.

Over a thousand miles away, the headquarters of the Polish army in Iraq was based in the region of Khanaqin-Qizil Ribat, close to the Iranian border in the rocky desert of the Tigris basin. Transit camps had been set up in various

The coat of arms of the Kossakowski clan that dates back to 11th century.

Right: Dad in a school photograph when he was seven years old.

Below: The boarding school at Suwalki on the eastern border.

Above: The family photograph; back row: Roman and Stanislav, front row: Boleslaw, Camilla and Czeslaw.

Below left: Camilla Kossakowski.

Below: Waclaw Kossakowski, 1938.

Top of page: Cadets in the army from September 1st to 17th, 1939. Dad is fourth from the right on the back row.

Left: At Warsaw University with his roommates when Dad (far left) was 19 years old.

Top of page: Dad standing on the left amoungst the Army cadets in the Suwalki forest region.

Middle: Waclaw kneels (front left) with the other cadets in the Suwalki region.

Bottom: Waclaw travelling with the 1st Survey Regiment. Basyl Lerowiecz is 2nd from the right.

Top of page: Tatiszczewo propaganda photograph showing a pot of fish soup being made.

Middle: Tatiszczewo propaganda photograph for a news report. These people were dressed well and told to smile and be happy by government officials.

Bottom: Tatiszczewo, the south Russia resettlement camp in 1941. When released due to the 'amnesty', Dad was taken to this camp. This is a propaganda photo showing Dad walking through the trees.

Left: The insignia badge of the First Artillery Survey Regiment showing the Vistula mermaid.

Above: Consecration ceremony at the entrance to the Polish cemetery at Monte Cassino, 1st September 1945.

BO TO JEST MOJE MIA

Above: The Kotwica 'anchor', the symbol of the Polish Underground and the Home Army (Armia Krajowa) painted on a wall of the ghetto. The words translate as 'because it's my city'. The anchor comprises the two letters P and W merged into one (Polska Walczaca – Fighting Poland).

Opposite page and overleaf: Area maps of Monte Cassino (5 KDP, Fifth Kresowa Divison).

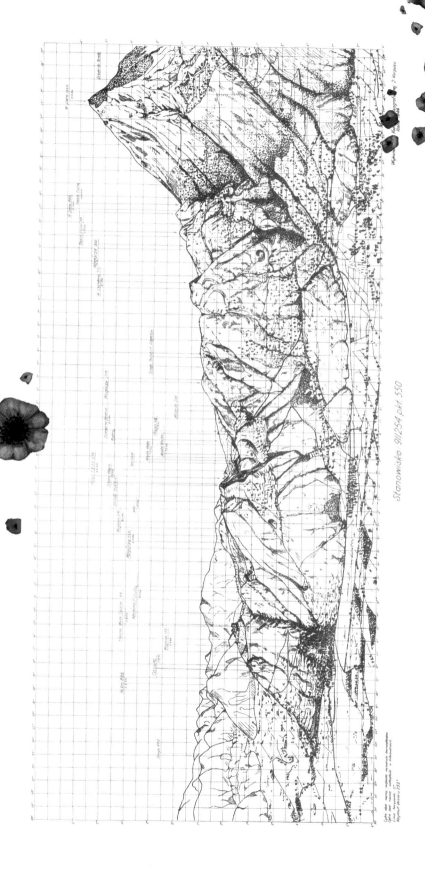

Stanowisko 9II/254 pkt. 550

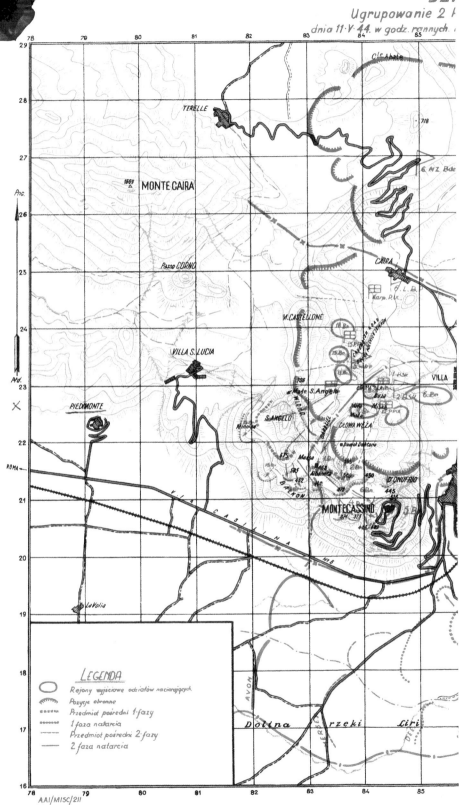

LEGENDA

○ Rejony wyjściowe oddziałów natarcia jących
Pozycje obronne
Przedmiot pośredni 1·fazy
1·faza natarcia
Przedmiot pośredni 2·fazy
2·faza natarcia

MONTE CAIRA

TERELLE

Passo CORNO

V.CASTELLONE

VILLA S.LUCIA

PIEDIMONTE

S.ANGELO

GŁOWA WĘŻA

MONTECASSINO

D'ONUFRIO

CAIRA

VILLA

La Volia

Dolina rzeki Liri

ROMA

Png.

Płd.

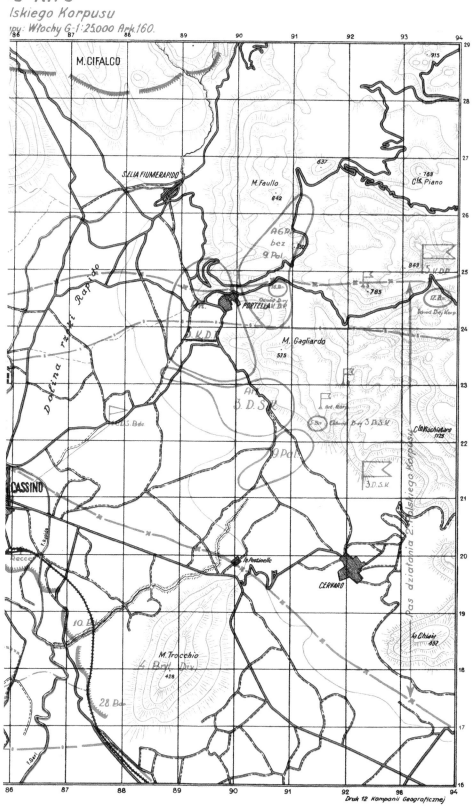

M. CIFALCO

S.ELIA FIUMERAPIDO

M. Faullo
642

637

C. Piano
763

915

A6P.
bez
9 Pal

849   5 U.DP

16 Bn

Odwód D-ry
PORTELLA D.P.

785

17 Bn
Odwód Dcy Korp.

D.K.D.

M. Gagliardo
575

Dolina rzeki Rapido

Ar.
3.D.S.K.

Art. Rdz.

C.la Vischiataro
1125

U.S.Bde

3 Bn   Odwód Dcy 3 D.S.K

9 Pal.

3.D.S.K.

CASSINO

F. Rapido

Recce

le Pastinelle

CERVARO

Pas działania 2. Włoskiego Korpusu

la Chiaia
452

10 Bn

M. Trocchio
428

4 Bryt. Div

28 Bde

F. Gari

KORPUS OSOBOWY

Stosunek do służby:

artyleria .

rezerwa

9 B

Nazwisko i imię *KOSSAKOWSKI WACŁAW-PIOTR*

Czesław i Kamila Kropiewnicka.

Mianowany podporucznikiem w PKPR dn. 26.4.47

ZESZYT EWIDENCYJNY

P/8889

I. LISTA EWIDENCYJNA

II/12/47 z dn. 26.4.47

Stopień: *podporucznik*

Starszeństwo: 1 kwiecien 1945 - *ROZK. PERS. 2 KARP. Nr 120/45.*

Lokata:

PRZYNALEŻNOŚĆ SŁUŻBOWA	STANOWISKO ZAJMOWANE
1 Putk Pomiarowy Artylerii.	dubluje dce plutonu 1 baterii topo-graficznej

POLISH
8889

		dzień	miesiąc	rok
1		*19*	*maj*	*1919*
		miejscowość	powiat	województwo
		Milewo-Żółtki	*Wysoko-Mazow.*	*Białostockie*
2		a) *rzym — kat.*	b) *polska*	
		samotny.		

			nazwisko panieńskie i imię	wyznanie	narodowość
2	Stan rodzinny	Żona			
		Dzieci (imiona i daty urodzenia)			

Dad's identity card for the resettlement camp in England, 1947/48 showing his division, First Artillery Survey Regiment, Topography Battalion. The other details include his birthday, 19 May 1919, his religion Roman Catholic and where he was born.

Wzór 27.

R *1919.*	Kat. zdrowia	„H"		

KOMENDA UZUPEŁNIEŃ	L. Karty ewid.	UWAGI:
w Polsce *mi pumedt.*		
w Z.S.R.R. *K.U.Nr. 4*		
w *Iraku K.U.Nr.3*	*131./III*	

ZESZYT EWIDENCYJNY

NAZWISKO *KOSSAKOWSKI*	
IMIONA *WACŁAW PIOTR*	
STOPIEŃ wojskowy	Data awansu (degradacji)
Kapral podchorąży	*28 II 42*
podporucznik rezerwy artylerii	*1. IV. 1945.*

Uzgodniono 6.VI.1945 O. Pers. 2 Korp.

Left: Evidence of leaving the Polish Army in 1945, showing dates and places. At the top is Russia (Z.S.S.R.) and Persia (Iraku/Iraq) and beneath his rank on leaving – Corporal in the First Artillery Regiment.

Below: 'Demob' papers from the British Army showing his new address in Nottingham after leaving the resettlement camp.

Form PRC/D. 1

APPLICATION FOR FINAL TERMINATION OF SERVICE IN THE POLISH RESETTLEMENT CORPS AND A.T.S. (P.R.S.)

13

To:—The Officer in Charge,
    Polish Resettlement Corps
      Record Office,
        Witley, Surrey.

(Number) *Polish/8889* (Rank) ... *2/Lt.* ... (Name) *KOSSAKOWSKI* *22* (Initials) ..*W.P.*
                                                   (IN CAPITALS)

(Former Unit) ...... *453 B.U. P.R.C.* ......

(Permanent Address) .. ~~Tec~~ *TECHNICAL COLLEGE,*
(IN CAPITALS)   *SHAKESPEARE STREET, NOTTINGHAM.*

Condition for Termination of Service.

    1. Three months in Civil employment on the unemployed list or, on Class "W" of the Reserve of the Polish Resettlement Corps. (Give date of Relegation) .....*14. 10.* 19*47.*

    2. I fully understand after termination of service:—
    (a) That I have no further call or connection with the P.R.C. or A.T.S. (P.R.S.) and cannot return to it.
    (b) I will receive no further assistance from the Polish Resettlement Corps either for emigration or repatriation.
    (c) That, on final termination of service, I must report to the Civil Police and have my Police Registration Certificate endorsed.
    (d) If I require any assistance I will have to apply to the appropriate Civil Authorities, e.g., Ministry of Labour, Ministry of Health, Assistance Board, etc.

    3. *Application.*

    I wish to apply to terminate my service in the Polish Resettlement Corps, I fully understand the conditions under which this will be granted and enclose A.F. W 3044 (Polish).

PUBLISHED
P. II. O.

(Signature) ...... *Kossakowski*

(Date) ...... *21. 11. 1948.*

(B47/358) 100000 10/47 W.O.P. 28470-2

Army Form X204 (Polish)

ALIEN IDENTITY CERTIFICATE
DOWÓD OSOBISTY OBCOKRAJOWCA

POLISH RESETTLEMENT CORPS AND A.T.S. POLISH RESETTLEMENT SECTION. RELEGATION TO
THE UNEMPLOYED LIST OR TO THE RESERVE FOR EMPLOYMENT APPROVED BY THE MINISTRY
OF LABOUR AND NATIONAL SERVICE

POLSKI KORPUS PRZYSPOSOBIENIA I ROZMIESZCZENIA ORAZ POLSKA SEKCJA PRZYSPOSOBIENIA
I ROZMIESZCZENIA (A.T.S.). PRZENIESIENIE NA LISTĘ, NIEZATRUDNIONYCH LUB DO REZERWY
CELEM PODJĘCIA ZATRUDNIENIA ZATWIERDZONEGO PRZEZ MINISTRY OF LABOUR AND
NATIONAL SERVICE

Number/ Numer ewidencyjny P/8889	Rank/Stopień 2/Lt.	Name (Block Capitals)/Nazwisko (litery drukowane) KOSSAKOWSKI Wacław Piotr	
Date of Birth Data urodzenia 19.5.1919	Height/Wzrost 5 ft. stóp 5,5 ins. cali	Colour of hair/Kolor włosów fair	Colour of eyes/Kolor oczu blue
Complexion/Cera dark		Marks or scars/Znaki szczególne none	

Address to which proceeding/Adres miejsca przeznaczenia

The Alexandra Hotel, 7, Gregory Boulevard, NOTTINGHAM.

Occupation/Zawód student	Employer (name and address)/Pracodawca (nazwisko i adres) Technical College, NOTTINGHAM.
Ministry of Labour occupational Classification No. (if known) Numer zawodowej klasyfikacji Ministry of Labour (jeśli znany)	Date of relegation for an indefinite period Data przeniesienia 14. 10. 1947

Local Office of the Ministry of Labour and National Service
at which he/she will report   Employment Exchange
Miejscowy Urząd Ministry of Labour and National Service   NOTTINGHAM.
do którego winien/a się zgłosić

A. I CERTIFY that the above named alien has been relegated from military service to the Unemployed List/Class " W "
Royal Army Reserve*. He/She has been instructed to report to the Police on his/her arrival in
NOTTINGHAM
..............................and thereafter to the local office of the Ministry of Labour and National
Service.

STWIERDZAM, że wyżej wymieniony obcokrajowiec został przeniesiony ze służby wojskowej na Listę

Niezatrudnionych/do Rezerwy.* Został/a on/a pouczony/a, że z chwilą przybycia do .....NOTTINGHAM.........
ma się zgłosić do Urzędu Policyjnego, a następnie do miejscowego Urzędu Ministry of Labour and National Service.

Date/Data 13. 10. 47	Signature of Officer Commanding Podpis Dowódcy Oddziału O.C. 453 BASIC UNIT P.R.C. Lt.Col.

B. I understand that, with my consent, I have been relegated to the Unemployed List/Reserve* from the Polish
Resettlement Corps/A.T.S. Polish Resettlement Section* in order that I may take up work with the employer specified
above or such further work as may be approved by the Ministry of Labour and National Service. I understand

Identity paper showing Dad employed by
Nottingham University and his temporary address.

ID card with photograph showing his address of where he stayed in Nottingham at the time. This had to be carried at all times and shown whenever he was asked.

NUMBER

RMA. 7276363

SURNAME
KOSSAKOWSKI

CHRISTIAN NAMES (First only in full)
Waclaw P.

CLASS CODE
A.

FULL POSTAL ADDRESS
7. Gregory Boulevard, Nottingham RMA

HOLDER'S SIGNATURE
Wacakowski

CHANGES OF ADDRESS. No entry except by National Registration Officer, to whom removal must be notified.

REMOVED TO (Full Postal Address)
42 Parkdale Road, Nottingham RMA

REMOVED TO (Full Postal Address)
22. Seely Road, Nottingham, RMA

REMOVED TO (Full Postal Address)
2, Parkdale Street, Nottingham RMA

REMOVED TO (Full Postal Address)
41, Vernon Avenue, Wilford. Lot RNS

REMOVED TO (Full Postal Address)
27 Manville Close, Bankdale Rd. Nottingham

FOR OFFICIAL ENTRY ONLY (apart from Holder's Signature). MARKING OR ERASURE, IS PUNISHABLE BY A FINE OR IMPRISONMENT OR BOTH. ANY OTHER ENTRY OR ANY ALTERATION.

Left: Dad and Mum's wedding day in Derby, 1951.

Below: Vadek and Irene on the confirmation day in 1964 at St. Joseph's Catholic School at Stanford-le-Hope, Essex. In front are we three daughters – identical triplets – from the left Lyn, Sharon and Irena.

Left: Dad outside the family home in the mid-1970s, before it was knocked down and a bigger one built. Alongside is Tadek Kossakowski his nephew.

Middle and below: Threshing hay on the farm in the early to mid-1970s.

Left: Roman, my uncle,
with his wife Henja
and Tadek, their first
born and above with
Tadek's sister, Ella.

MR. KOSSAKOWSKI

The chance Britain gave him

FIFTEEN years ago Wacław Piotr Kossakowski, of 20, North Parade, Derby, was a prisoner of war in Russian hands. To-day he learned from the Textile Institute that he was one of 18 new Associates they had elected.

First "ray of hope" for Mr. Kossakowski was in 1941, when he left a prison camp after Russia had come into the war, to join the Polish Army which was being formed.

He fought with a Polish unit in Italy with the Eighth Army, and came to England when hostilities ended, gaining a scholarship to Nottingham University under the scheme to help Polish ex-Servicemen.

WORKS IN DERBY

While a full-time student at Nottingham from 1946-50, he gained the higher diploma in textiles, and since 1950 he has been employed as a dyer by W. Lowe (Derby) Ltd. at their Stuart Street works.

Mr.

Above: Roman and Henja with my father in 1966/7.

Left: A local newspaper cutting from the late 1950s (?) recounting Dad's study and work in textiles.

Above: From left to right: Henja, my Mum Irene and Dad's Mum Camilla Kossakowski.

Right: Dad with me on the family farm in 1997, the last time he was there.

Left: The statue of King Zygmunt III in Castle Square of the Old Town, Warsaw.

Below: Warsaw trams in 1989.

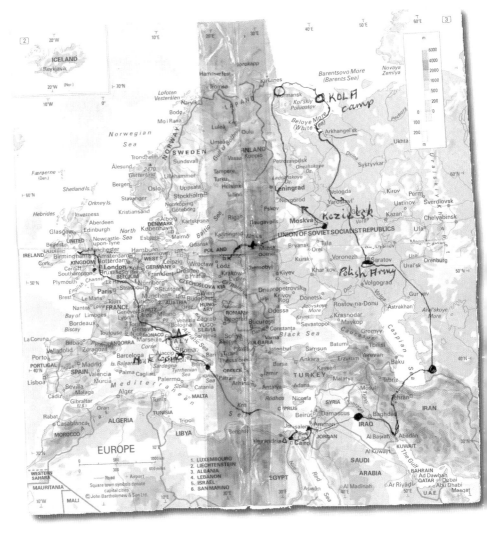

This map was included with Dad's letter (shown on following pages) to his grandson Darren in 1991 for his history assignment at school. The camp Kola, is ringed (top right) and marked on the map is Dad's journey from Moscow to Kola through Persia across the Caspian Sea, Italy, and eventually to England.

10/2/91

Dear Darren,

Thank you for your's two letters. I am so glad you did so well at school getting a star and certificate.

I like your's writting, it's much better than your's Mum, at least I can read it easily. So carry on like this

This is my life story.-

1939. I was studing mathematics at Polish-University at Warsaw. When war started on 1st Sept. I joined the Army fighting Germans but on 19th we were captcieved by Russian Red Army. As a prisoner of war I was ~~kept~~ hold at camp at Kozielsh near Moscow Then we were transported in cattle coaches to Murmansk near North Pole

It took seven days and nights, then by boat two days to a labour camp KOLA. Because it is so close to North Pole so sun shines all the time in Sommer and in winter there is no sun at all, only North Lights. We were building runways for russian military aeroplains, living on ray bread and fish soup, and ground was frozen ~~enough~~ even at sommer.

At June 1941 Germans attaced Russia and Stalin released all Polish prisoners of war to join free Polish Army near Saratow. which latter moved to south of Russia near Iran.

At Spring at 1942 we left Russia for Iran and to

Iraq where we received
English equipment and arms.
My camp was about 50 miles
from Baghdad in desert
where we trained all summer
1942 and it was very hot.
In november we moved to
Palestine where I went to see
Jereusalem and other Holy
places. On Christmas day we
moved to Egypt near Cairo
and I went to see Pyramids,
In february 1943(4) we were
transported by boats to
south of Italy to fight German's Army again.
May 1943(4) the battle of Monte
Cassino, where in 5 days
German's in concred bunckers
killed 2000 polish soldiers
and wounded many others.
I was lucky in arkilery

shooking guns two miles from front line. After that we were slowly pushing Germans north. May 1945 my guns were shooting to Bologna when I was told that war finished. I had chance to visit Rome and some other places. Polish Army couldn't go back to Poland, because Communist Russia occupied all my country, so 100 000 Polish Army came by train and boat to England. After demob I went to Nottingham Technical College where I got Higher Diploma at Textile as a Dyer. There I met my wife Irene and married her at Nottingham First I got job at Derby

then at 1957 I got job
of chief Dyer at British
Bata Shoe Co. at East
Tilbury from which
I retired at 1984.

So it is short story
of quite long my life.

Dear Darren if you
would like more details
may be I can tell you
when I see you later.

Love
Grandad.
Waclaw Kossakowski

P.S. I enclose a map that
will help you to follow
my life journey.

Left: Warsaw University – Dad's last visit in 1977.

Middle: Raking hay on the farm in 1989 with my cousin Tadek and a neighbour.

Bottom: Hitching a ride in the farmyard in 1997. Three-year old Ryan, Dad's grandson, and Roman (who was 79) with the milk churns.

Left: Dad with grandson Ryan, 30 months and great granddaughter Chelsea (18 months). Dad was 83 when this photograph was taken.

Below: Dad celebrating his 85th birthday with grandson Ryan.

Dad meeting the Polish Pope John Paul II
in the Vatican City, 1987.

Campaign Stars, Clasps and Medals

A thorough and comprehensive assessment of entitlement using the record of service has been completed. Your full and final award in recognition of service in the war of 1939-45 is enclosed.

NUMBER OF STARS, MEDALS, CLASPS OR EMBLEMS ENCLOSED	4

Order in which the awards should be set up eg for framing	Description of Ribbon	Clasp or Emblem (if awarded)
1. 1939-45 Star	Dark blue, red and light blue in three equal vertical stripes. This ribbon is worn with the dark blue stripe furthest from the left shoulder.	Battle of Britain or Bomber Command
2. Atlantic Star	Blue, white and sea green shaded and watered. This ribbon is worn with the blue edge furthest from the shoulder.	Air Crew Europe or France and Germany
3. Air Crew Europe Star	Light blue with black edges and in addition a narrow yellow stripe on either edge.	Atlantic or France and Germany
4. Arctic Star	A central vertical stripe of white flanked on either side by a thin stripe of black and then three equal stripes of red, dark blue and light blue.	
5. Africa Star	Pale buff, with a central red stripe and two narrower stripes, one dark blue, and the other light blue. This ribbon is worn with the dark blue stripe furthest from the left shoulder.	8th Army or 1st Army or North Africa 1942-43
6. Pacific Star	Dark green with red edges, a central yellow stripe, and two narrow stripes, one dark blue and the other light. This ribbon is worn with the dark blue stripe furthest from the left shoulder.	Burma
7. Burma Star	Dark blue with a central red stripe and in addition two orange stripes.	Pacific
8. Italy Star	Five vertical stripes of equal width, one in red at either edge and one in green at the centre, the two intervening stripes being in white.	
9. France and Germany Star	Five vertical stripes of equal width, one in blue at either edge and one in red at the centre, the two intervening stripes being in white.	Atlantic
10. Defence Medal	Flame coloured with green edges, upon each of which is a narrow black stripe.	Silver laurel leaves (Kings commendation for brave conduct, Civil)
11. War Medal	A narrow central red stripe with a narrow white stripe on either side. A broad red stripe at either edge, and two intervening stripes in blue.	Oak Leaf

The Under-Secretary of State for Defence

(Armed Forces) presents his compliments

and by Command of the Defence Council

has the honour to transmit the

enclosed Awards granted for

service during the war of

1939-45

Medals awarded to Dad – in the middle is the Monte Cassino Cross. The others are for the Italian Campaign – two Italian Stars, a Defence and a War medal.

The Kossakowski house as it is today.

locations, many almost one hundred miles apart with communications only possible by radio and courier; Vadek's base camp was located fifty miles or so from Baghdad.

Faced with a sea of sand and no trees in sight, General Anders described his rather basic, new headquarters as: 'Several primitive huts surrounded by a sea of tents pitched on sand.'

For the travel-weary Poles, the new challenges they faced were enormous, and the dramatic change of climate was only one of those many difficulties. The transition would prove problematic and painful for all of them; Vadek felt as though he was in a state of limbo.

The men were drained. Spirits long crushed by both physical and mental abuse resulted in deep psychological scars, causing many to wake in the night screaming from vivid nightmares as they relived the horrors and brutality at the hands of the Russians. Some found simple communication difficult, being unable to voice any concerns, or even to speak freely for fear of a savage blow from the butt of a rifle in the face or back.

At the same time their bodies had to battle against malaria and other disease epidemics. Many were quarantined with typhoid and yellow fever; many suffered from scabs and sores from unwashed bodies and the filthy clothing worn for so long that it had become almost a part of them.

Large canvas tents had taken the place of cramped timber huts and there was plenty of good food to be had, with field kitchens serving cooked food the like of which Vadek had never seen before; and he was amazed at such a choice. Eggs, bacon and sausages, tomatoes and baked beans. Porridge or Weetabix. And all this just for breakfast!!

Everyone suffered terribly from dysentery, while the lack of fresh fruit and vegetables had resulted in a deficiency of Vitamins A and C, causing night blindness and scurvy.

Vadek was not alone in having so few teeth that he could not chew properly, and he was fitted with false teeth by the British dentist. He had a very small appetite, for his stomach had shrunk and was full after just a few mouthfuls. Which unfortunately, usually came up again soon after being eaten.

Fortunately, there were field hospitals with medical supplies and antibiotics, and for the first few months the doctors were extremely busy. Sadly, this care came too late for those who had suffered from severe frostbite; toes or fingers, maybe both, were lost. Vadek was fortunate, for though his feet were discoloured and caused intense pain, they recovered over time with the proper care and treatment; even so the treatment itself, though simple, was extremely painful.

Hair was shaved and the filthy rags, threadbare army greatcoats and lice-ridden fur hats were burned, to be replaced with lightweight uniforms: crisp cotton shirts and cool khaki shorts.

And there were showers! With warm water! Never had Vadek been so happy to see a bar of soap! The simple luxury of being clean, of *feeling* clean, had so long been denied him. After years of washing outside using snow and putting back on the same filthy clothing which crawled with filth and decay, the wonderful sensation of a shower and the luxury of clean clothes was something Vadek relished for a very long time to come.

Having endured the terrible conditions in Siberia and being denied so much for so long, even the simplest things seemed luxurious – but the ex-prisoners had left one dreadful extreme for another, and it was very difficult for them to acclimatise.

Here the air, often above 50°C, felt like a furnace, almost unbearable after the intolerable cold of the Kola Peninsula, which had often fallen below –50°C. It was hard to tell whether the blazing heat outside was worse than the heavy oppressiveness inside the tents; Vadek had never before felt air so thick it was like walking into a wall.

Then there were the sandstorms. So quickly they would come. Huge billowing clouds of stinging, suffocating sand, sweeping down from the horizon and enveloping everything in seconds. The winds whipped the sand into a swirling, furious frenzy, stinging and burning wherever they found unprotected bare skin and getting into ears, eyes, mouth. A sandstorm would overturn jeeps, rip up tents and leave a trail of destruction in its wake.

It was impossible not to compare everything to the wretched conditions of the previous camp. The huts and bare bunks were now replaced by tents and comfortable camp beds with clean cotton sheets. These were surrounded by mosquito netting and raised several inches from the floor, preventing scorpions from sharing them with an unwary soldier. Even so, every night Vadek checked his bed and every morning shook out his boots.

But the most important difference was the wonderful sense of freedom. Freedom to talk without fear. No more beatings, no humiliations. Vadek and his compatriots were treated as men, as equals. Vadek had feared in the prison camp that he would die as a nameless number, frozen to death and discarded when no longer of any use. Now once more, he had his name back.

The Polish army in the east was reorganised several times, and now Vadek was part of the Ninth Field Artillery Regiment; a division of the Fifth Infantry and an independent part of the British Eighth Army. The Poles were given British equipment, and when the men were well enough they underwent intensive training and field exercises, including extensive practice with heavy artillery.

At first, the camp was a hive of activity with tents being erected and supplies unloaded, but once it was set up, the men settled into a routine and became better able to cope with the demands of their training.

Vadek was given the opportunity to continue with his studies and sent to a military cadet school in Tehran for several months. Here, he acquired the highest qualifications possible in topography, geo-science, mathematics and astrology.

On his return he became an instructor of topology to the junior cadets, where his skills were put to good use overseeing general manoeuvres and commanding several divisions of the artillery regiments. His previous understanding of Italian and German enabled him to teach basic commands in both of these languages to other military personnel in readiness for the Italian campaign. At the same time he was promoted to an officer; and it was in the officers' mess that he met Basyl Lesowiec, who would become his close and lifelong friend.

Despite Vadek's command of several languages, English was not one of them and he, like the other Poles there, found the language – necessary for life in the camp – difficult. At the end of each day, it was always a relief for them to converse in their own language, and Vadek more often than not could be found in the officers' mess with Basyl.

Surrounded by their fellow countrymen, with the general hubbub of Polish conversation in the background, Vadek gave a deep sigh as he added sugar to his tea: 'It's so good to be able to talk without having to think about what I'm saying. Always I have to think and think. The concentration gives me a headache! And by the time I've thought of the word, everyone has forgotten what I'm talking about!' He stirred his tea, jabbing the slice of lemon around in it. 'And when I think I know a word, someone else says it differently!'

'I know exactly what you mean,' said Basyl. 'Here we are having a cup of tea, but some of the men call it char and others say 'do you want a brew?''

Vadek nodded. 'But some I can't understand at all! Have you heard of a place called Scotland? They're British. And I'm told they speak English – but I can't understand a single word they say!'

'But some speak English and I have no idea what they mean!' Basyl responded. 'What does 'Cor blimey' mean? Or 'luvva duck'? Why was our training officer talking about ducks when he was showing us how to load a rifle?'

Vadek laughed. 'I don't know. Maybe he was feeling hungry.' He took a spoonful of the tinned peaches he had saved for these evening chats. 'Mmm, these are good. Better than duck.'

They both laughed. It felt so good to laugh. But then Vadek went suddenly quiet and looked sombrely at his friend.

'I never thought I would laugh at anything again, I almost feel guilty when so many have died.' He remembered Thomask. And the officers … and the many frozen dead he had buried. And he knew he could never forget.

The heat was something that had to be endured, just as the cold had had to be endured. There was no choice. Vadek often asked himself which he preferred, for they could both burn and they could both kill. But he was unable to answer, for they were each as terrible as the other. He only knew with absolute certainty that he would prefer to be in Poland.

Physical fitness had never been one of Vadek's strong points and he resented being forced to train in the sweltering heat. In the early morning and again in the late afternoon when the heat was not so intense, there would be the dreaded PT. This meant press-ups, bending and touching toes, squats and running.

It was something he hated with a passion, even more than cleaning and polishing his boots at the end of each day, when they were coated with a fine film of dust.

Early morning, and already the shimmering heat of the desert could be felt as Vadek joined his friend for breakfast in the canteen tent. Basyl was already seated there, staring morosely into his tea, listlessly stirring the sugar. He barely looked up as Vadek greeted him.

Noticing Basyl's full bowl of porridge, Vadek asked, as he placed his plate of eggs on the table: 'Your stomach not feeling happy? I know as soon as I'm thinking I might want something, mine starts to complain again.' He peered closely at the two soft eggs sitting on his plate. 'I'm not even sure I want these; I'd rather have a tin of peaches.'

Basyl stopped stirring but remained silent, his grey eyes focused on his tea. 'Is it the heat? Is the heat getting to you? It does me. I just want it to rain. And I hate PT – far too hot for all that jumping about. Now that's enough to put anyone off their food.' He smiled, 'Reminds me of school, and I didn't like it then, either!'

Basyl looked up, rather bewildered: 'What?'

Vadek turned and looked at his friend. 'I thought it was the heat …or PT … but …' he paused, concern in his voice, 'What is it? What's the matter?'

Basyl stared into his cup again, a distant look on his face, 'I was thinking of Poland and my family.'

Vadek slowly moved the eggs around on his plate, then pushed it away without touching it. 'I know what you mean,' he said quietly. 'There isn't a day I don't think of mine. The not knowing where they are … or what's happening … are they alive or dead?'

'That's just it,' Basyl continued, his head buried in his hands. 'I do know. And sometimes I just can't bear it. They're all dead and there was nothing I could do.'

His voice dropped to barely a whisper and Vadek had to lean to catch his words: 'I should have been there. Maybe I could have done something, helped them. Or died with them.'

Vadek was dumbfounded. He wanted to say something to comfort his friend, but knew he could not. He placed a compassionate hand on Basyl's shoulders, and they sat there in silence.

Vadek knew that Basyl came from western Poland, but other than that he knew very little. Like everyone else they never spoke of what had gone before; it was too distressing, too painful. No one was ready to face the unimaginable horror that each had experienced; far better to block it out and never speak of it. Each and every man there had gone through their own personal hell.

He did not know what had happened to his own family, if they were alive or dead; but because he did not know, he had hope. And hope was what kept him going, kept pulling him out of that dark abyss of despair. To have nothing … no one left at all. How did one keep sane? He did not know.

Yet another sun-drenched morning; not yet 8 am, but already almost 30°C. Scanning the endless hard blue of the sky, Vadek wished for a rain cloud. Or any cloud.

Finishing his toast in the shade of the canteen tent and seated opposite his friend at the trestle table, Vadek remarked, 'I've had enough of PT. I'm not doing it today.'

Basyl looked up at him, a spoonful of porridge suspended en route to his mouth: 'Why? Are you ill?' He studied Vadek's face. 'You don't look ill.'

'I will be if I do PT. It's far too hot. And I'm very pale under this tan; can't you tell?' He swallowed the last of his tea before saying thoughtfully, 'And it does always aggravate my knee, though no one can tell me why. Cover for me?'

'You know it'll go on your record if you're found out,' Basyl said, finishing his porridge.

'Well, I'll have to make sure they don't find out.' Vadek said, then placing a hand on his stomach and winking at his friend, he lurched forward with a groan. 'Ooh, I feel sick,' and he moaned again, a little louder this time.

'Someone's coming. Don't overdo it,' Basyl said as he helped him to his feet.

A tall British officer strode over. 'Now then,' he said briskly, 'What's going on here? You all right, lad?'

Vadek let out another groan but said nothing and just gave a feeble nod of his head.

'He just feels sick,' explained Basyl who had thus been drawn into Vadek's little scheme.

'Get yourself off to sick bay then; they'll take care of you. This blasted dysentery is a nightmare for you Poles. The doctor will soon sort you out.' And off he marched, straight and tall, hands behind his back, to the medical tent.

'You've had it now,' Basyl whispered. 'He'll know for sure that you're faking it. Your acting isn't that good. What were you thinking of?'

Vadek sighed, 'Well, I was hoping he might just send me to my tent. I should have thought of a better plan. Next time, I'll put more thought into it. Perhaps I should say I have heatstroke!'

And so it was that Vadek received his one and only punishment during his time in the army, noted on his records: 'For evading physical training. He was given ten days' confinement to his tent, cleaning boots.

As the Polish troops recovered during that summer it was decided to transfer them to Palestine by the end of the year. Several units had already been deployed to the mountain passes along the Iranian border, and to the northern oil fields of Iraq. Here they would complete their mountain training, in preparation for the terrain they would encounter in Italy.

Vadek at last had the rain he craved, for now it was early November and the start of the rainy season. Welcome news reached the men of several victories by the Allied troops in north Africa, including the final battle for El Alamein. 'Operation Lightfoot,' a massive bombardment launched against Rommel in late October, had forced a German retreat and their complete withdrawal by 4 November. This ended the Axis presence on the continent; and it gave the Poles some hope for what the future might bring, lifting spirits that had long been crushed.

Meanwhile, Hitler was also losing the hard-fought battle for Stalingrad which had begun that summer, for although the Germans had reached the outskirts of the city in early September they had been forced to entrench, waiting for supplies. This loss of momentum would cost them dear, as they were then held back further by the early onslaught of a particularly severe Russian winter – and by the determination of Stalin to defend his namesake city. He had told his army, 'Not one step backwards. Whatever the cost.'

Hitler was of the same mind and refused to let his beleaguered troops withdraw, despite the fact that his army were forced to eat their horses to avoid starving.

Concurrently, Vadek was on his way to Gaza, Palestine, a journey of several weeks in tarpaulin-covered trucks over rocky desert, passing through Jordan. It was an uncomfortable journey, bumping for hours over the rough tracks of the remote uplands on narrow, hard seats, but Vadek never complained. After all, what could be worse than what he had left behind? There would never be anything he would complain about after that.

And he was free. Free to fight for his country. No longer was he just waiting to die; he could die while fighting for Poland.

Reaching Jerusalem in early December, the men erected their base camp on the outskirts of the city and were given a few days' leave. With the onset of winter, the cooler weather Vadek used this opportunity to explore some of the amazing sights he had read about in the books from his school in Suwalki, at the time never imagining that he would one day be able to see them for himself.

Brought up in the Catholic faith, Vadek found the Holy City of special interest. Each religious site held significance for him, though all the buildings showed the marks left by different centuries and previous cultures. He found it fascinating to visit the Mount of Olives, the Temple Mount and the Tomb of David, and wished he was able to write home, to tell his mother he had walked the same path as Jesus had trod on the way to the crucifixion; she would never have believed it possible and so would be truly astounded. Though he enjoyed such wonders, his joy was dimmed by the fact there was no one to tell of all that he saw, nor to see their amazed looks at the telling. So for Vadek, each new experience was tinged with sadness.

A few days later, the camp was struck. Another five hundred miles were covered before reaching Cairo in Egypt, land of the Pyramids, the final staging post before deployment to Italy.

It was 25 December 1942 and Vadek enjoyed his first free Christmas for years, sitting in the shade of the sphinx with the pyramids as a backdrop. He never forgot that day, that Christmas. So very different from the past three Christmases spent in prison camp, each torturous day the same as the others and never knowing what day – or even what month – it was. Now for the first time in several years, he felt alive.

Later that Christmas Day, the spirits of the men were high as they sang songs around the open fire. In the desert, night-time temperatures can drop well below freezing even in the summer months, but Vadek found that even the sunshine-filled days of winter were tinged with an icy breath from the mountains, and the odd shower of rain could fall.

The Christmas Day music came from an accordion player, while another man played a harmonica. Some of the Scots danced a reel, occasionally tripping over one another's feet and sprawling into the sand. Poles from the mountains of Zakapane, not to be outdone, demonstrated their traditional highland dances, leaping high over rifles laid on the ground, and then others not so skilled, tried to do the same … As the evening wore on, the songs were replaced by quieter ones, making everyone's thoughts turn to home.

Vadek fingered the photograph still in his pocket, for he carried it with him always. What kind of Christmas were they having? He knew they would be thinking of him this day, just as his thoughts were with them, and he could only hope they were all safe and well.

He remembered the last time they had been together. He could still see Ana's face as she came across the farmyard, her hair blowing out from under her scarf, and her blue dress, patterned with so many white daisies it looked almost white, flapping gently around her legs.

Time had not diminished the memory but rather had made it sharper, for memories of happier times were all there were. He saw Ana so clearly in his mind's eye it was almost as if she were really there, reaching out her hand to him just as she had done that day.

It was a Sunday; more often than not it was a Sunday when she visited. After helping his mother wash and tidy up after the meal, Ana had retired to the main room where Vadek was playing with Roman, who left him to sit on Ana's lap; he liked Ana, and squirmed and laughed out loud when she tickled his tummy.

'You're a *pączek* and I'm going to eat you up!' she said and opened her mouth with a big growl, making him curl up his legs and squeal with delighted anticipation.

Camilla suggested it would be a good time to go for a walk, as it was time for Roman's nap, and he would never settle if he thought Ana was going to eat him. So she carried him off to the bedroom, though he protested with gusto. Ana smiled at Vadek and went to fetch her scarf, while he waited outside, chatting to his father.

Czeslav was busy in the workshed, replacing the worn-out sole of a shoe with a piece of cut leather from another old one; nothing was ever wasted and a use could always be found for everything.

He acknowledged Ana with a nod when he saw her crossing the yard to join them. She had tied a small blue scarf round her face and it accentuated her rather dainty features, though did little to prevent the breeze ruffling her hair. She smiled at him, but her eyes were on Vadek.

'Always did like blue,' commented Vadek's father as he continued with his task, and the tapping of his hammer hitting the nail into the heel could be heard on the wind as they walked together; out of the farmyard and along the track.

Finding contentment in each other's company, there seemed little need for words and as they walked, Ana shyly put her hand in Vadek's. With no particular place to go, hand in hand they walked slowly towards the edge of the village.

Perhaps if he had known that peaceful day would be their last together, he might have said something. Maybe. He wasn't sure. But with hindsight he certainly wished he had, because all he had now was a memory. A memory of a perfect day with the girl he loved. And he would never have that time again.

TEN

KAPICE, SPRING 1943

ONE DEATH IS A TRAGEDY, A MILLION IS A STATISTIC.

JOSEF STALIN

The Russians were coming. From across the Ukraine and the Baltic, the steppes of Mongolia and the frozen tundra of Siberia, they came in their thousands, spilling into Poland through its open borders.

Column after column of straggling, weary soldiers; most on foot, some on horses and in carts. They were a sorry sight, haggard and dejected, with famished faces and glassy eyes staring straight ahead, limping on bloodied feet bound with cloth, bedraggled in their dirty, tattered uniforms. And hungry, always hungry, for the Red Army had the Germans on the run after they had surrendered at Stalingrad in early February 1943, and Stalin pushed his troops hard.

The sleepy village of Kapice lay just thirty miles inside the Polish border and its inhabitants could do nothing to prevent the Russians' relentless march. Here, as in many other places, the invaders forced the inhabitants to leave their homes, commandeering the dwellings for their own purposes, some as resting places or even makeshift hospitals. Although both Russians and Poles were now fighting the Germans, the Russians cared little for the suffering of the Poles and took what they wanted.

Many of the Polish men and older boys had left to fight in the free army or were hiding in the forests with the Polish Underground movement. Czeslav had left shortly after the start of the war and Camilla was, like so many others, left alone with her small children to fend for and survive as best they could.

She had not heard any news of Vadek for several years, and did not know if he was alive or dead. Every day for many months, Roman had asked, 'When is Vadek coming home?' Now he no longer asked.

Forced to leave her home to the occupancy of the Russian soldiers, she knew her family's only chance of survival was to move into the bunker. From outside the bunker resembled a rabbit warren, the walls made of earth covered with turf; it had been used for storing food during the winter. It was some several hundred yards distant from the farmhouse, almost on the perimeter of the farm. Now, it made a simple but claustrophobic dwelling, for it gave them protection from the rain, with just a tiny hole at one end to let in a narrow shaft of daylight and some air. The air inside, always stuffy, became damp and chilly when it rained, and mud poured like custard down the walls. The floor, waterlogged, left nowhere dry for them to sleep or put their few belongings, and it was impossible to ignore the hundreds of insects crawling throughout the bunker; which found their way inside clothes and into hair.

Camilla put branches and leaves on the floor in an attempt at making a bed for her children, but nothing stayed dry for long. With no sanitation or water, and no heat or light, Camilla often felt she was at her wits' end and would cry in frustration at the unfairness and hopelessness of it all. But it was an existence, and they were alive.

Ana had come to say goodbye. The early morning low-lying cloud had turned into a fine drizzle as she walked the several miles to Kapice. She shivered occasionally, for her thin jacket did nothing to dispel the damp or provide any warmth. Her sandy hair seemed darker, for it was plastered to her head, making her small features look even smaller.

Russian soldiers had occupied her home too, and so she and her mother had decided to leave for the town of Lumza, a four-to-five day walk through the forests. Her mother's sister lived there, and in the perhaps forlorn hope that there would be some shelter there, they were moving.

It was an emotional farewell. Camilla had grown very fond of Ana and the feeling was mutual. Now she felt that she was losing not only a dear friend and confidante but the daughter she had never had.

Sheltering under a large and leafy tree, they talked for some time; of the war and the constant fear one felt and the loss of loved ones. And of course, of Vadek. For both, there had been no time to say their goodbyes, and there were many things left unsaid to the person they both loved. Each tried to console the other, and give reassurance that they would meet again.

Camilla reached into the pocket of her skirt and pulled out a small photograph. Though rough and slightly torn at the edges, the main image was still clear. It showed Vadek with a large group of children, taken at summer camp many years before. Tenderly, she stroked the face of her son as, choking back a sob, she told Ana how much he had enjoyed those times at camp. How he returned home full of stories of sleeping in tents and eating meals around the campfire while singing songs. Was it really so long ago?

As they both looked at the little Vadek, his cap askew and a shy smile on his face, their eyes brimmed.

'Take it,' said Camilla. 'It will give you hope. Please.' She took Ana's hand and gently pressed the photograph into her open palm, closing the fingers on top. They clung to each other for several moments, both loath to let go, for who knew when they would see each other again?

Then straightening up they faced each other, their sorrow mirrored in their eyes. With a little smile, Ana turned away and began to walk back the way she had come, the rain mingling with her tears.

SPRING 1944

Food was always scarce; Camilla was forced to scrabble in the frozen ground with her bare hands for a few mouldy potatoes, digging up and boiling roots, anything she could find to feed Roman and Stanislav. Nettles, chopped up finely and boiled in water, made a nourishing drink, though at first Stanislav had spat it out in disgust. Sometimes she would venture a little further from the village, hoping to find something, anything, to prevent her children from starving.

Today she had walked further than usual, and had now reached Jakub's house. She looked sadly upon the once beautiful house and garden where he had lived with his wife and son, and which they had so lovingly tended. Wistfully she remembered their greetings on the way to church.

So much had happened and so much had changed. Now the garden was run down and overgrown, and only weeds flourished. They covered the ground where once vegetables had grown so abundantly, and smothered anything that tried to grow. Nothing was left. Everything destroyed. The house, too, had been ransacked and was now a shell with its windows smashed and furnishings broken. On the door, half-hanging on its broken hinges, could be seen a faded yellow Star of David.

A shudder ran through her thin body as she remembered what had happened, and unwanted memories came flooding back. How shops and businesses were destroyed in Bialystok if they were owned by anyone Jewish. No Jewish person was safe. Poor Jakub had been dragged from his shop and thrown into the street. The window was smashed and everything in his little watch repair shop broken. Destroyed or looted. Then they had set about him; he was so badly beaten that he was hardly able to stand upright before being driven away in a large black car with blacked-out windows.

He had not been seen since. Distraught, Jerzy and his mother had fled their home. No one knew where they had gone or what had happened to them.

A tear slowly rolled down her dirt-streaked face. She stood there, alone with her memories. She remembered with startling clarity the morning when they had come to the house. She had just lit the stove and put the kettle on to boil for tea, when she heard a commotion in the yard. Before she could even cross the room and look through the window to see what was happening, they had battered loudly on the door, waking her sons. She was shoved back roughly against a wall with her boys, fear a tight knot in her stomach as she had held them close while they screamed in terror at the strange men with guns ransacking their house.

Trying to keep calm for the sake of her children, she had begged the soldiers to allow her to collect a few things, and so in just a few moments she had quickly pushed some warm clothing into bags and grabbed some blankets. But when she tried asking for food, they had laughed cruelly and shoved her outside, almost pushing her down the steps as she stumbled through the doorway clutching her bags and her children. For a few moments she had stood there, confused and shaking, Stanislaw and Roman clinging tightly to her skirts, crying loudly, unable to understand what was happening. And she was frightened, so very frightened, for it had been truly terrifying and she knew they could easily have been shot.

The whole fabric of her life was torn apart and she could not think. But she must, she must. Still shaking, quivering with shock, she forced herself to be calm, to collect her thoughts from the chaotic jumble in her head and to think rationally. Clearly. Where to go, what to do. Think. Think. And she thought of the bunker.

Now at last, when the worst of the winter was over, the Russian soldiers had gone. They had eaten the chickens, but they had kept the cow for her milk, and they had left her behind. This probably saved the lives of Camilla's family. But the soldiers had taken the horse and cart, piled high with blankets, utensils and wounded comrades.

She had waited so long for this moment. To be able at last to return to her beloved home, all she had dreamed and prayed for during the long, horrendous months, but now … she was hesitant. She had schooled herself for this day, tried to prepare herself for the scene of devastation she knew would await her; but now it was actually here. She chided herself for being foolish then bracing herself, she strode across the farmyard and up the steps. But she faltered as she faced the half-open door. Then slowly, tentatively, her hand reached out and pushed, forcing the door to open fully on its rusty hinges.

It took a second for what she was actually seeing to register; the magnitude of the devastation was almost too much for her to comprehend. She stood there, rooted to the spot for several seconds, staring in disbelief at the scene in front of her.

Slowly, without conscious thought, she stepped inside the doorway. For some moments she didn't move, her eyes adjusting to the light before venturing further into the room. The air was foul and stale, heavy with the smell of urine. She stared in disbelief and horror, for it was incomprehensible to her. Did they not have families, homes they wanted to return to?

She willed herself to walk around, her eyes not wanting to see, her mind not wanting to accept. Slowly she ran her finger along the edge of the carved pine dresser, leaving a trace in the dust. It had been made by her husband Czeslav for their first wedding anniversary, and had little hearts cut into the two shelves and in the two doors which were now broken. The shelves inside were empty and all their contents strewn onto the filthy floor. Broken plates littered the floorboards and rubbish was strewn everywhere; even bloody wound dressings. Treasured items telling of happy times, such as photo frames and pictures, were all smashed. There was nothing of any value that had not been destroyed.

As her eyes slowly moved around the room, they rested on a small wooden carving lying in a corner amidst the filth. She picked it up and wiped it on her threadbare woollen skirt to remove some of the grime. It was a stork, standing on one leg. Camilla stared at it, and as she looked upon the simple but beautiful little carving made with so much love and care by her son so many years before, the tears began to fall. All the pent-up emotion that had been held back was released and she screamed.

A heart-wrenching scream that echoed throughout the empty house, as if her soul was being ripped from her body. Until, with all her emotions spent, she sank to the floor, sobbing quietly. Her world was falling apart all around her and there was nothing she could do to stop it.

How long she sat there she didn't know, but the sound of feet scurrying across the yard and a small voice crying for his mother jolted her out of her despair and brought her back to reality.

'Roman! Stanislav!' She called out to her sons with a lighter tone so as not to upset them, and straightening up, she smoothed down her skirt and pushed the stork deep into her grubby apron pocket. Wiping a grimy hand across her tear-streaked face, she put on a brave smile and held out her arms to the two children she still had with her, and gathered them close.

She had to carry on. She had to be strong, for she still had a family, and one day they would all be together again. She was sure of it. This was their home, and no one was going to take it away again.

It was several weeks since the Russians had left, and there had been no word from Ana. Camilla missed her, and often felt consumed by despair and loneliness. There were so few people left in the villages. The men and older boys were fighting, either in the army or with the resistance, and only the women were left to try and carry on. Others had simply disappeared or been taken away by the secret police. She had no knowledge of Czeslav's whereabouts, only that he was working with the resistance. It was better not to know. Talk was dangerous, and careless talk cost lives.

Many of the farms and houses were derelict and falling into disrepair, their fences used for firewood. Fields once abundant with crops were overgrown and untended. The once lively communities were now eerily quiet with only the occasional barking of a starving stray dog, or the doleful bellowing of a cow needing to be milked. The life and soul of the village had been destroyed and only the empty shell remained.

She remembered the autumn of 1941, when the Germans had moved into the area, beating back the Russians. Whenever there had been any kind of resistance, reprisals were swift and brutal. Whole villages were sometimes wiped out or several villagers picked at random and executed. Camilla lived in fear that one day she or her children would be next. So many had died, and there was no one in the neighbourhood who had not lost someone.

She remembered sadly how they had come for Henja's brother, Tadek. Unable to fight due to a war injury, he was one of just a handful of older children in the village and was in constant contact with the resistance fighters hiding in the forests.

Soldiers had come to the village where Henja and her family lived. With all able-bodied men either fighting in the military or part of the resistance movement, there were only women left behind with the sick and elderly. And children.

The peace of the day had been broken by the sound of cars speeding along the lane on the outskirts of the village. Tyres screeched to a stop and car doors slammed, as a German officer briskly stepped out and shouted orders to the soldiers now jumping down from the trucks behind. They darted in all directions, small dogs yapping noisily at their heels, disturbed by the sudden and unusual commotion in the usually sleepy village as the soldiers ran through the narrow streets holding their rifles in front of them. Banging loudly on closed doors and kicking them in if no one answered, they dragged the frightened occupants outside and forced them to move quickly to the centre of the village.

Humming to herself, Henja had been busy hanging out the washing in the sunlit garden. She stopped as she heard the cars, shouts and heavy boots. The sheet fell to the ground as she turned swiftly and ran towards the house, screaming for her mother and brother.

Tadek was in the woodshed, chopping logs for winter. On hearing the shrill sound of his sister's screaming, he paused in mid-swing. Axe still in hand, he raced towards the house, but stopped abruptly when he saw the soldiers running across the yard. Maybe he could get one of them he thought wildly, but with that same instant thought was the sober realisation that the other would then shoot not just him, but his mother and Henja as well. Slowly, he placed it on the ground.

With frightened faces the family clung together in bewilderment and fear as two soldiers with rifles burst into the garden, roughly forcing them forward as they were ordered to move quickly ahead and into the street.

Every single person had been ordered out of their home and herded to the centre of the village No one was spared. If a villager was unable to walk, they were dragged from their bed.

When everyone was assembled, the officer spoke curtly and dispassionately. He informed them that in retaliation for the attempted murder of a German general by the Polish resistance, the people of Poland would be severely punished and every male over twelve years of age would be shot. Then he gave a nod to the waiting soldiers, who immediately strode across to anyone matching that description, and shoved them against the church wall. The villagers watched helplessly, horror on their faces, sadness in their eyes – for what could they do against so many guns? This had happened before, for this is what they did and no one was safe from the brutality of the Nazis, and they could only silently watch and pray.

As a soldier grabbed Tadek, his sister screamed and clung to him. 'No!' she sobbed hysterically, 'Take me! Take me!' But she was swatted away like a fly, and fell backwards to the ground.

Tadek felt dazed, not fully comprehending and was gripped by fear. He began to shake uncontrollably though he tried desperately to control it. His slight frame faced forward; on one side of him was an old man, cap on head leaning on a stick, on the other the local blacksmith, injured by a kick from a horse many years before.

Both faced forward, resigned to their fate, knowing if he ran he would be shot immediately and another would be taken in their place. What could they do but stand bravely, proudly? Tadek prayed he would be that brave.

The Germans were readying their rifles … only a few seconds of life left … he searched for Henja among the small crowd of villagers who were forced to watch or be shot themselves. Many of the women were fingering their rosaries, mouthing silently as they prayed. Others crossed themselves and men held their cap in hands, heads bowed, pity and sorrow in their eyes.

He saw Vadek's mother, Camilla, quietly sobbing, arms protectively around her children; Stanislav was in her arms, his little hands clinging tightly around her neck, and Roman clutching her skirt, hiding behind it. Both not understanding but fear etched in their faces, sensing that something terrible was happening.

He remembered the many times he had gone to the house, to eat, to play, to work.

As he stood there, waiting to die, with his life in the hands of the German soldiers, time seemed to slow down, and he felt a sense of unreality.

The scent of mimosa wafted on the breeze, birds were singing sweetly and the storks were feeding their young in their nests on the chimney tops and barn roofs. Bizarrely, he wondered how they never overbalanced on their long, spindly legs.

He had always loved the springtime, with the new life all around. Should one die on a warm spring day when it felt so good to be alive?

Should he blame the resistance fighters, so many brave men and women who risked their lives every day and often died under terrible torture?

No. They all did what they had to do and he would do it all again, despite the cost. A quiet pride surged through him as he stood there, back against the wall, staring death in the face.

He focused on Henja, tears streaming down her face, eyes pleading, imploring, begging them not to shoot. Sobbing and screaming she flung herself at them again, pummelling them with her tiny fists and no thought of her own safety. But they only laughed at her with no hint of compassion in their eyes, until her mother dragged her away, fearing they would both be shot.

'Please Henja,' she said, 'please don't let me lose you too.'

He remembered how they had played together, laughed together, and fought each other as siblings do, loving and hating each other.

A sudden longing for life, a life he had taken for granted before, surged through him with an overwhelming tide of indescribable emotion; for it was going to be taken away from him, and he did not want to lose it. A tear rolled slowly down his cheek. He did not brush it away.

As he gazed upon the face of his sister, they looked at each other for what seemed a long moment in time but was barely a passing second, and he knew he wasn't alone. A feeling of calm came over him, the shaking stopped. He stood bravely for their sake, to show he wasn't scared any more. He wanted to tell them it was all right. To not be sad.

His mother's face was the last thing he saw as a volley of machine gun fire riddled his small body and peppered the wall behind him.

The noise shattered the day; it stopped the birds singing, and the stork, startled, flew from its nest. Camilla would never forget the horror of that day; it was seared in her memory forever.

SUMMER 1944

Little Stanislav was sitting by the side of the track and digging in the dust. He was annoying the beetles by flipping them over and tossing them up in the air, laughing if they landed on their backs, waving their legs.

A few yards further sat Roman, his thin face streaked with dirt and brow furrowed in concentration as he scratched his name in the dust with a stick.

'I've done it. I've done it,' he shouted, beaming with delight. 'Mama, Mama, Come and see!'

He stood up and started to run – straight into the legs of a Russian soldier. The force knocked him backwards onto his bottom, where he sat and began to howl, partly with indignation and partly in fright. Camilla heard her son yelling, and dropping all the berries gathered from the hedgerow in her apron, she ran the short distance and grabbed him. Hugging him close, she glared fiercely at the soldier in front of her who seemed to be just as dazed as her son was.

'I'm sorry,' he said in Polish. 'It was not my fault, I meant no harm.' He spoke barely above a whisper and he looked, despite the bulk of his uniform, as frail as a stalk of grass bending in the wind.

As Camilla looked upon his shattered face, she felt a tug of compassion and her eyes softened. Despite the ravages of war, he looked no older than Vadek. He too has a home and family somewhere, she thought sadly. As the soldier really seemed to notice her for the first time, a spark of recognition lit up his vacant eyes then died as quickly as it had come. He shuffled forward, moving painfully on blistered, bloodied feet, leaning heavily on his rifle.

'Wait,' she called out, not really knowing why. 'Tell me your name.'

He stopped, turning slowly to face her again. 'Marek,' he replied.

ELEVEN

TO ITALY, 1944

FOR OUR FREEDOM AND YOURS, WE SOLDIERS
OF POLAND, GIVE OUR SOULS TO GOD, OUR LIFE
TO THE SOIL OF ITALY, OUR HEARTS TO POLAND.

BOLESLAW KOBRZYNSKI, MONTE CASSINO
CEMETERY OBELISK, 1944

In June 1943 the Polish troops were officially redesignated the Second Polish Army Corps. Now, with the red Vistula mermaid on his shoulder, Vadek was in the First Artillery Survey Regiment, overseeing manoeuvres by his unit and part of the field artillery division.

The designation was a proud moment for all Polish soldiers – but just a month later, on 4 July, came the news of the death of General Sikorski. On leaving Gibraltar, seconds after take-off, his plane had crashed into the sea. It was he who had initiated the Sikorski–Mayski agreement for the amnesty of Polish prisoners, and his untimely death was a severe setback to the Polish forces.

Elsewhere, the success of the invasion of Sicily by the Allies, which had begun on 10 July 1943, had far-reaching political consequences for Italy, as it would ultimately result in the removal of the increasingly unpopular Mussolini. On 25 July, with the approval of Victor Emmanuel, the king of Italy, Mussolini was sent to an isolated jail in the Abruzzo region. Six weeks later, on 10 September, Italy officially surrendered to the Allies. On 12 September, Mussolini was rescued from his mountain-top prison by German Special Forces; however, on 13 October Italy declared war against Germany.

While these events unfolded, the date was being set to begin transferring the Polish Corps to Italy. The first units were to be mobilised on 15 December, and the movement was to continue until 1 April 1944. Preparations for the journey from Egypt began, and more and more equipment arrived as the deadline fast approached. There would be three field artillery regiments deployed to the Italian peninsula, and Vadek's division was to be one of these, under the command of General Nikodem Sulik.

The men were restless, eager to move on and fight the enemy, and Vadek was excited to hear his unit would be mobilised in mid-February 1944, departing from Alexandria for the Italian port of Taranto. He had no qualms whatsoever about leaving the Middle East, with its desert and heat, and enthusiasm shone in the eyes of the men, for they were on their way to Europe and could now prove themselves ready for battle.

Travelling on open boats within a convoy, there was always the threat from attack by German U-boats, which forced them to zig-zag through the open waters while within sight of the African coastline. At the same time, they had to keep a lookout for mines below and enemy aircraft above. Occasionally a shout from a sailor on watch indicated the sighting of enemy planes – but for the most part these ignored the troopships, being more concerned with the huge assault ships carrying tanks and artillery.

Days at sea stretched into almost three weeks, which seemed far longer in the awful conditions. With no proper sanitation or washing facilities, the thousands of men, squashed together on boats meant for just a few hundred, slept where they stood.

The weather became stormy. Almost all the soldiers were seasick. But seasickness was something Vadek did not suffer from, and he volunteered daily for lookout duty, thankful for time on deck where he could breathe deeply despite the miserable weather. With his rifle over his shoulder, the sound of his whistling as he kept watch, in his vain attempt to drown out the groans of the men below, was whisked away by the gale.

It seemed an interminable time before the men arrived at the foot of southern Italy and disembarked at Taranto, one of the ports which had been captured by the Allies. Though the soldiers were landing on a hostile shore, they all felt relief and gratitude to be on solid ground once more, and pushed northwards with a lightness of step despite the steady drizzle.

The next day rain and hail greeted them, and that evening as the temperature dropped the rain became sleet, stinging the cheeks into a rosy pink – but nothing like this could dampen the spirit of the Poles as they marched on.

Progress was slow as they passed through destroyed towns and villages and along blown-up roads that were crowded with enormous concentrations of Allied forces. Soldiers of every nationality and country: American, Canadian, British, French, New Zealanders and more. All trudging in seemingly endless columns, and all of them converging on Monte Cassino.

The small, once picturesque town had been flanked by meadows full of poppies. Now it was a decimated wasteland of burnt earth with not a single blade of grass to be found, and only the blackened stumps of trees protruding from the ground. Overlooking the Liri Valley, Monte Cassino was in a mountainous region surrounding Rome some eighty miles to the north-west, and formed a crucial part of the German defences known as the Gustav Line.

Situated on an 1,100-foot peak, Monte Cassino guarded the main approach to the capital, and was of prime strategic importance to the Germans, who had positioned themselves high up on the rocky terrain. The Gustav Line had been prepared and fortified by the Germans long before the Allies had arrived, and was a formidable obstacle. Now it was defended by fifteen divisions of the German army, who were able to see everything that was happening around and below their many near-inaccessible vantage points. Heavy artillery had been sited in many caves, and well placed machine-gun posts were dotted all over the peak, along with mines and miles of barbed wire. German snipers had positioned themselves in the relative safety of their concrete bunkers and in the many caves dotted about on the higher levels, and so were easily able to pick off anyone climbing up from below. The Germans were in total control of the area and were familiar with every treacherous path.

The unseasonal weather made the terrain almost impassable. Torrential rain had caused rivers to flood and tracks were washed away by torrents of mud brought down from the mountains. This hampered the movement of vehicles and troops. Essential supplies were washed away in the rivers of thick mud which snaked their way along the narrow, winding roads. Jeeps and trucks had to be pulled free with ropes, time-consuming and physically draining. New roads and telephone lines were repeatedly constructed by the engineer divisions and supplies were carried in by hand or on mules.

The historic monastery of Monte Cassino was perched high on a hill, and dominated the town which was still patched with dirty grey snow. Founded by St. Benedictine in the sixth century the monastery had been a place of worship for Christians from all over the world, but now, under daily artillery attack, had been all but destroyed.

Despite Allied attacks on Monte Cassino several months earlier, the town was still in German hands. The first assault on the line had begun on 4 January 1944 by American and French forces; but such was the situation with the Germans in their secure, well positioned bunkers and their familiarity with the terrain, no progress had been made by early February. An American soldier later wrote, 'Long snaking tracks with 30 degree incline made us dizzy. We were living in another world where we can resist sleep, hunger and thirst. Only coffee keeps us going, maybe thirty cups a day.'

A second assault, with the Americans replaced by Indians and New Zealanders, was made later that same month; but this assault met with the same problems as the first and fog had hindered movement as well. At the end of the second offensive, despite great courage shown by the Allied forces, the position of the Germans on the ridge and in the town remained unchanged.

Early on the damp morning of 15 March the third battle began. The ground attack was preceded by bombing on the town and on the German positions on the hill. American tanks then made their way along the roads cleared by engineers, but along the mountain passes they were forced into single file; anti-tank mines caused a block that held up the assault in the now torrential rain.

The German forces had the huge advantage of shelter in bunkers or caves, and though they suffered terrible losses too, they were able, with reserves, to regain their positions at the base of the monastery when the bombing stopped on the evening of 19 March.

For three terrible months the Allies, with Gurkha and New Zealander troops at the forefront, continued to assault Monte Cassino, suffering hundreds of casualties, but the German paratroopers repulsed every attack. The New Zealanders held on to their position in the town until their armour was destroyed, forcing them to abandon their positions, and the Gurkhas, cut off from their supply lines and under heavy fire, were forced to retreat from Hangman's Hill and Monastery Hill.

During the course of the third battle, talks were held on 21 and 24 March between the British Eighth Army commander, General Oliver Leese, and the US army commander, Mark Clarke. They discussed the situation with the Allied Armies' commander in chief, Sir Harold Alexander. They were acutely aware that things were not going their way. So a change of strategy was deemed necessary, and the decision was taken to approach Monte Cassino in a flanking action.

It was decided that the Second Polish Army Corps would be assigned to launch a fourth battle from the northern flank, with divisions of the British Eighth Army to the left and Tenth Army to the right. They would together break through the German positions on Monte Cassino to capture Monastery Hill and take the town of Piedimonte, a strong point on the Hitler Line, a fall-back defence behind the Gustav Line.

A further plan of action was put forward on 3 April, stating that the Poles' artillery units would destroy the German positions on the hill, in preparation for the infantry assault on Monte Cassino.

This would happen in two stages; first the monastery, and second, Piedimonte. The artillery would cover the advance of the Third Polish Carpathian Rifles from the north and the west, along with the other Polish divisions and Allied forces. The fourth assault was scheduled to start on 11 May at 11 pm.

On 5 May, briefings were held on communication between the Third Carpathian and the Fifth Kresowa divisions and their artillery units, which would oppose the German artillery. The infantry would advance behind an anti-artillery barrage, their two main objectives Phantom Ridge and San Angelo. Both assault parties would be covered by artillery fire from the Piedimonte area and other strategic locations. However, the ground the infantry was to cover was a death trap, filled with land mines, booby traps and barbed wire.

Three days before the battle, a service for the Roman Catholic Poles was given by a chaplain from the Third Rifle Battalion. Vadek knelt there in the relative serenity of his immediate surroundings, bathed in the gentle warmth of the early morning sun, struggling to push its way through the hazy cloud layer on one of the few relatively dry days of late spring. A wispy mist still clung to the surrounding hills and layered the valley. A stab of emotion scorched through him as he remembered so vividly the Sundays at his local church with his family. He glanced across at Basyl, head bent, hands clasped, in silent meditation. What thoughts must be going through his mind, for he no longer had a family – and Vadek was filled with deep, empathic sadness for his friend.

The shelling of the Liri Valley and the isolation of Monte Cassino monastery were of paramount importance. Vadek's artillery regiment was positioned along a wide sector of hills two miles distant in the Piedimonte region, providing cover for the attacking infantry and tank regiments. In the weeks preceding this fourth assault by the Poles, the artillery divisions with their supplies had to get themselves into position, an exceptionally hazardous procedure due to the narrow roads which were mostly little more than tracks. Steep gradients with hairpin bends and sheer precipices proved treacherous for the trucks, which were totally unsuited to the terrain, and even for the jeeps. It was a slow and laborious process, made even more difficult by the blackout. The men wore white crosses on their backs, and a man wearing a white towel would walk in front of the convoy to show the way.

The evening before on the ridge was relatively quiet, with spasmodic bursts of fire and the occasional thunder of artillery shattering the silence, echoing in the still night air. Vadek was in his makeshift shelter. The rain beat down noisily on the tarpaulins, running off their open sides onto the mud, forming puddles and rivulets. It was difficult to find a dry spot, and Vadek was cold and damp. His thoughts turned to Andrzei. He had heard nothing of his cousin and was filled with sorrow at the thought of possibly never seeing him again. He stroked his chessmen and wished he could play one more game. This time, he thought with a little smile, he might even let Andrzei win, though it was rather funny watching him lose; he got so mad!

'Vadek! Vadek!' His mind must be playing tricks; pre-battle nerves he told himself, as with a shake of his head, he began to pack the men away into their tiny carved box.

'*VADEK!!!*' Startled by the voice almost in his ear, he dropped the box, the contents spilling out. His mouth dropped open; he couldn't believe it. Surely he must be imagining things. But it WAS Andrzei! A thinner, even scrawnier Andrzei, but Andrzei none the less. The rain was dripping off his helmet down his neck and onto his face – which had a grin from ear to ear. 'Well, little cousin, aren't you going to invite me in?' he asked, stooping under the tarpaulin and stepping into the relative dryness of the shelter.

In an unfriendly country torn apart by a bitter war, the enemy always only one step behind and never knowing if the day you woke up would be the day you died, the joy of seeing someone you knew and loved was immense. Vadek was overcome. Too tongue-tied to speak, he opened and shut his mouth like a fish, and his eyes brimmed with tears.

Hurriedly, he wiped a hand across his eyes, 'This dammed rain,' he muttered as he put two wet arms around his cousin and enveloped him in a bear hug that threatened to break his ribs. For a moment they just held onto each other, for no words could capture how they felt and neither wanted to let go for fear of losing one another again. The relief at having found one another was so great!

They talked long into the night, Andrzei filling in the details of what had happened over the years. He explained how he had been left for dead on the outskirts of Warsaw after his tank had hit a mine, but had been rescued by the Underground movement and cared for until he had been able to join his tank regiment once more. Then like Vadek he had been transferred to Italy, eventually arriving here in Cassino. 'With so many Poles here,' he concluded, 'I knew I'd find you if I searched long enough!'

He also told Vadek of a brown bear named Wojtek ('joyful warrior'), which had been adopted by the Twenty-Second Polish Infantry Division in Iran, that decided to help out by carrying ammunition, and was now its mascot. 'Maybe,' Andrzei said, glancing at the scattered chessmen, 'he'll give you a game of chess. So,' he added, 'how do you fancy being beaten?'

Andrzei returned to his unit, ready for the assault later that day. As he left Vadek's shelter, he turned and said, 'Keep firing those guns, little cousin; just make sure you hit the Germans and not me!' Then he was gone.

TWELVE

MONTE CASSINO, MAY 1944

WE DO NOT BEG FOR FREEDOM — WE FIGHT FOR IT.

ZYGMUNT AND LEOPOLD HARR 1944

On the night of 11 May, British and Polish fighter bomber squadrons continuously dumped explosives onto their targets below; 1,400 tons of bombs were dropped on the town of Cassino. Thousands of guns blasted the darkness like thunder, shaking the earth and lighting up the sky like a terrible firework display. The Allied artillery bombarded the German positions with over 2,000 shells in the first forty minutes, in preparation for the advance of the Polish infantry, and the Second Polish Corps artillery barrage continued until 1 am on 12 May.

The Polish infantry advanced with the field guns, facing a hail of machine-gun fire that scythed them down like cornstalks. Shells screamed overhead, the ground trembled and the air quivered, such was the power of the onslaught. The infantry could not always keep up with the artillery, confused by the rocky terrain and poor visibility from gunfire and smoke; tripwires set off smoke canisters, blinding, choking, and automatic machine-gun fire. The men crawled forward, lying flat, searching for cover – but the boulders had been blown to pieces by their own artillery and there was little protection for them. Desperately fighting for every foot of ground, often in hand-to-hand combat, there were heavy losses as the Poles were pushed back by the Germans from their bunkers at the base of the monastery. It was a massacre and the Allies gained no ground.

Radio and telephone communications were intermittent at best, as the shelling had damaged radio stations and telephone lines were cut almost as soon as they were laid. So communication depended on couriers.

From his vantage point on the craggy hillside, Vadek could see the horror unfolding in front of him as he continuously fired and loaded the heavy guns, blasting the enemy below. It took mathematics and pinpoint precision to hit the targets, and he was always conscious of Andrzei at the front line, perhaps in his line of fire – the tanks were pushing forward, firing their cannon into the bunkers, trying to break through the German line.

The German artillery were directing their fire at the Polish artillery, just as the Polish units were directing theirs at the Germans. It was a perilous situation to be in. Shells rained down on the gunners; flying debris exploded mines, showering the men with shrapnel. The noise was deafening.

Vadek was covered in debris; his helmet and face grimy, and coated with dust and myriad fragments of rock. The air, thick and heavy with smoke from the non-stop shelling, made his eyes feel like sandpaper, and he coughed harshly, choking on the hot, acrid dust.

A shell exploded nearby. Rocks, earth and shrapnel flew into the air, showering men and guns, cutting skin, severing arteries, overturning guns. Vadek was blown off his feet. Reeling, dizzy and a little disorientated, he shook his head fiercely, trying to regain his senses as he picked himself up, with no thought other than to keep on firing.

Frightened? There was no time to be frightened; no time to think. Perhaps, if he stopped. But he did not stop.

And always there was the rain. The ceaseless, torrential rain which meant that every step was a fight with the mud. Mud which resembled thick, stodgy porridge. Cold and clammy, it clung to the fibres and seeped into clothes, weighing down the hobnail boots, making each dragging step an effort to wrench the foot free. Bodies lay where they had fallen, and with no time or men to move them the stench was terrible. All the soldiers were in a pitiful state. There was no time to sleep; no water or sanitation, and with no proper medical treatment they were patched up where they lay, wallowing in the mud.

A Polish soldier later recorded: 'The company walked in slippers which came off quickly, many were barefoot, hurting their feet on the jagged rocks. It wasn't for lack of boots, but army boots slither and slide on these barren rocky hills and make it impossible to climb. Every man had a white cross painted on his back to help us find each other at night.'

On the morning of 12 May, a German paratrooper division launched a counterstrike against Phantom Ridge. It was rebuffed, but the ridge did not provide enough protection from the German machine-gun fire and artillery; resulting in many casualties.

In the gorge between Snakeshead and Phantom Ridge, the Poles advanced, pushing through rolls of barbed wire tangled up by artillery, under a constant rain of fire from the German bunkers that had not been cleared or had been retaken. The burned-out hulks of Allied tanks from earlier battles gave the Poles some cover from snipers; anti-tank mines had accounted for most of those tanks and they had been left on the hillside. Some still with their dead occupants inside.

The Fifth Kresowa Polish Division's push was hampered by mines and machine-gun fire. The troops had to cope with ever-increasing fire as they pushed through the murderous onslaught. When they reached the top, they threw grenades into the German bunkers, and fierce hand-to-hand fighting ensued. But few surviving Poles were unable to reach their main objective, for they were pushed back by German paratroopers who emerged from caves behind them.

The bitter fighting raged for several days with terrible loss of life to all combatants. The artillery shelled their way into enemy positions that had been located but not captured, and shelling continued, supported by the British troops and the Allied air force.

How Vadek survived each day, he did not know. It was almost surreal, as if he wasn't really there but only an observer and everything that was going on all around him was just a dream. It was a living hell of death and destruction, and Vadek could see no escape from the carnage and the screams of dying men.

The battalions were continually shelled by mortar and artillery. One of the shells hit a shelter of the Second Company, and a Polish soldier later wrote:

'An explosion killed the artillery radio operator and wounded an artillery observing officer. It killed the Commander; his face is a shapeless mass and his knee and arm ripped to shreds.'

The troops were being decimated, and with no reserves General Anders had no choice but to pull them back. Several units were evacuated from Phantom Ridge, enabling the German paratrooper reserves to return to their bunkers and reclaim their positions.

Anders was to say on reviewing the failed assault: 'There were not enough men; there were no reserves to take the places of the fallen. So many who fought so bravely after having survived the Russian labour camps had nothing to show for it. It is easier to capture some objectives than to hold them.'

The Allies paused to re-evaluate the situation and restock urgently needed ammunition and supplies. During the lull, in the relative quiet of spasmodic bursts of gunfire with only the occasional parachute flare, Vadek had time to rest and collect his thoughts while grabbing a much-needed bite to eat. Tugging a slightly dented tin from his inside pocket, he devoured the sardines inside. Though there were field kitchens or food trucks dotted about for the ever-hungry troops, they were not always readily available or easily accessible and it had been several days since he had last eaten a decent meal.

Huddled in the small muddy dugout, wet and cold, hugging his knees, he thought of the meals at home, the smell of baking and of course, a *pączek*. His mouth watered – it had been so long – and he smiled at the memory. Reaching inside a damp pocket, he retrieved his photograph and looked at the grainy image with longing.

This is what it is all for, he told himself. For them … and for Ana. For she was never far from his thoughts. Walking hand in hand with death every day, with only a few moments when his mind wasn't being bombarded with the chaotic, all-consuming sights and sounds of the battle, it was then that his thoughts would turn to home and his loved ones. For that was all any soldier had left to cling to; something to focus on and give some sense of reality. If that was lost, then there was nothing.

He found himself picturing the young woman he hoped to marry – if he managed to get out of this awful place alive, and if he survived the war, and if she hadn't forgotten him. There were far too many ifs, he thought disconsolately. If she was still alive … He tried not to dwell on that thought. It was too awful to contemplate, but far too often it strayed into his war-weary mind. He brushed it away; he was not going to think like that. He couldn't. Sometimes it was better not to think.

But if … *if* he had the chance again, he was going to ask her to marry him.

The sudden rattle of small stones and rocks jolted him bolt upright. Automatically he reached for the rifle that never left his side, while shoving the photograph back into his pocket, then heaved a sigh of relief as he realised it was Basyl. They shook hands warmly, for it had been some time since they had last spoken.

'Sorry to scare you like that,' Basyl said. 'I thought I saw you making your way here and decided to join you. Here …' and he passed a muddy and battered flask to his friend, 'have some tea – might not be too hot now, though, had it a while.'

Vadek took it gratefully; hot or cold it was a drink, and his own flask had been empty for some time.

'I can hardly recognise you, you're so covered with mud and dust. Even blood,' Basyl remarked with concern in his face and voice.

Vadek shrugged. 'Oh, that's nothing, just a passing mortar shell; the sky's full of them.' He looked at his friend, 'You too – muddy, I mean. Here you can't be anything else. Does it ever stop raining.'

It was a statement, not a question, and Basyl smiled. 'I remember all the times you prayed for rain in the desert.'

Vadek grinned. 'So I did, and I certainly have enough of it now!'

They sat in silence a moment, Vadek swigging the tea.

'What's happening your end?' he enquired.

'It's difficult to know; we're spread out.' Basyl stopped, then continued softly; 'The First Company over at Massa Albaneta were surrounded; their ammo was low and they couldn't get to their supplies; the flame throwers were down. They couldn't get into the bunkers …'

Nothing was said for several moments. Vadek offered the last of the now-cold tea to his friend, who shook his head. 'Any news of your cousin? I know he's with the tanks.'

'Yes,' said Vadek slowly. 'But I have no idea where. I do know there were some on the other side of the river, but they get bogged down in this awful mud.'

Swallowing the last dregs of tea and handing the flask back, he continued, 'It's difficult for tanks on these mountain passes, single file only, and there's the anti-tank mines …' He fell silent.

Shells screamed overhead, but in the dugout only their breathing could be heard as they pondered the fates of their comrades in arms.

'The war will be over soon; then we can go home. Won't be long now,' said Vadek hopefully but not very convincingly. Basyl didn't respond, and too late Vadek remembered his friend had no family to return home to.

'I'm sorry,' he began, but Basyl broke in: 'I want the war to be over as much as you do, you know,' and his face broke into a smile as he asked, 'What about that girl of yours?'

Vadek's face lit up: 'I want you to be the first to know … I'm going to ask her to marry me as soon as I get back home. And you're going to be my best man!'

'That's great news,' Basyl responded warmly, 'and of course I will! … but …' a grin spread across his tired features, 'she might say no. After all, who could put up with you for so long?'

Vadek laughed loudly. 'But how could she possibly say no?'

'How indeed?' said Basyl – and in that damp, dismal place with the sounds of war all around, the two friends laughed, bringing some much-needed humour into their dire situation. They were both young, yet they had suffered so much, witnessed so much, and both knew that neither of them might survive the war; and what they hoped would be might not be.

Basyl stood up and said simply, 'Good luck, Vadek.'

Vadek also rose, and they stared at each other for a long moment. No words were necessary. They both knew this could be their last meeting, for who knew which of them would be alive tomorrow?

As Basyl clambered from the dugout and into the open without a backward glance, Vadek suddenly felt intensely lonely.

'Good luck to you too, my friend,' he murmured.

On 13 May, two bridges for tanks and one for an Indian infantry regiment were erected across the Gari river – a dangerous task for the engineers, who were an easy target for enemy fire. The casualty rate was very high, but it was essential for the bridges to be built due to the terrible losses of boats carrying supplies and tanks. One bridge was destroyed almost immediately after construction. Nevertheless, four squadrons of tanks were able to cross the river that morning, and although many of them were bogged down as soon as they left the bridge, several made it through to the troops at San Angelo.

The next morning General Anders ordered another assault for two days' time. The assault, again preceded by artillery, would have the same objectives as before; taking the northern end of Phantom Ridge and San Angelo Ridge. Massa Albaneta was to be attacked by infantry and tanks, followed by an assault on the abbey.

On 15 May before the main assault, infantry moved in, covered by artillery. The Polish platoons came under heavy shelling, but though faced by a barrage of rapid machine-gun fire, the men of the Sixteenth Battalion charged at the bunkers, slinging in hand grenades as they ran. By 11 pm, they were in control of the northern end of Phantom Ridge.

Early morning mist and low-lying cloud slowed the arrival of armoured support, so it was decided to delay the assault until the early hours of 17 May.

General Anders issued documentation as follows:

- assault 06.00 hours
- counter-fighting artillery 06.00–06.20 hours
- artillery preparation 06.20–07.00 hours
- infantry assault 07.00 hours.

But other divisions were still engaged in heavy fighting, and the Fifteenth Battalion, under heavy fire, took the southern side of Phantom Ridge at 7.15 am despite serious losses. Meanwhile the men of the Seventeenth Battalion were climbing up to San Angelo, despite relentless volleys of machine-gun fire.

Their major later wrote, 'We bled there, just below the top, from dawn till dusk, unable to capture it. We and they lay there facing each other, slaughtering each other.'

Following them up the hill was the Thirteenth Battalion, but the Germans had easy shots from their vantage points and were able to pick them off, despite being hammered by grenades thrown into the bunkers at short range. The Thirteenth's major pushed forward undeterred to a bunker, grenade in hand, but was killed by a mortar shell. Shaken, his men lost heart and slowed, but their captain defiantly began to sing the Polish national anthem. As his voice rang out clearly, resolutely, the men rallied themselves, and picking up the tune they marched on with grim determination shining in their eyes. As shells zoomed past, their new commander, Major Jan Zychon, a respected intelligence officer before the outbreak of war, led the way, shouting encouragement to his men and refusing to keep down. He was soon killed. As he lay dying, his head cradled in a young soldier's hands, his face waxen and breathing shallow, he said simply, 'For Poland.'

By noon, many of the officers had been killed or wounded, so despite the deployment of the entire Fifth Division, only the northern slopes of San Angelo were taken that day.

A combined tank and infantry force won Massa Albaneta in the early hours of 18 May, but the southern slopes of San Angelo were still under German control; a battering ram assault gradually wore down the German defences to gain a strong point and push through the Line.

On the morning of 18 May, the Twelfth Regiment of Polish Lancers was ordered to take Monastery Hill. They succeeded. But after constant combat for several days, many soldiers collapsed at the monastery gate. Others, barely mustering the energy to push on, entered the monastery to triumphantly raise the white and red colours of the Polish flag above the ruins at 10.45 am. A soldier played the Krakow Hejnal, a well-known bugle call originally used to alert Krakow's citizens to impending invasion by Genghis Khan's Mongol hordes. Soon, alongside the Polish flag flew the British one.

Later that same day, another assault was launched on San Angelo, but it was met with strong resistance, and it was not until the early evening, with just a few small pockets of resistance left, that it was under the control of the Poles. By the morning of 19 May, the entire Snakeshead Ridge was in Polish hands.

General Nikodem Sulik was to write later that the heavy and bloody fight for Phantom Ridge, 'caused serious and long-lasting trauma to the Polish troops. The soldiers lost their most beloved commanders, their closest, immediate leaders of platoons and companies, they lost their closest colleagues and friends.'

After the terrible slaughter of so many soldiers and loss of hundreds of civilians, the Battle of Monte Cassino was over, and the road was now open for the Allies to advance to Rome. This was the beginning of the end of the German occupation of Italy.

Vadek picked his way slowly through the thousands of dead bodies that littered the ground. German and Poles lay together in death in the ruins;

bodies entangled, arms and legs sticking up like tree-stumps in a devastated wasteland. Torn and bloodied corpses wrapped in jagged barbed wire. Never had he seen so much death and destruction, and it filled him with horror and despair.

Sorrow engulfed his entire body. Then he closed his mind and hardened his heart to the sight and smell of the bloodshed, praying desperately that he would not find Andrzei's body here. Hoping against hope that his cousin had come through – as he himself had – and was merely wounded somewhere, waiting to be found. Andrzei had escaped death before; he could do it again.

Vadek convinced himself of this as he picked his way carefully between the men around his feet; some still groaning not yet dead from their wounds, but slowly dying with vacant, sightless eyes, staring, unseeing. Some reached up a feeble arm towards him as he passed – but there was nothing he could do, for they were already dead, but did not know it.

Bodies charred, burnt beyond recognition from exploding shells and mines, identifiable only by their dogtags. What if one of those blackened bodies was his cousin? The thought was too terrible to contemplate. He pushed it away, continuing to search, more hopeful with each dreadful step he took through that frightful sea of corpses.

Hope was an intoxication that buoyed up his spirit; he would find his cousin any minute now, and they would laugh and meet up later for a game of chess and everything would be all right again. Because he could get through this terrible nightmare of a war if he had his cousin with him. All he had to do was find him, and everything would be all right.

There in front of him was a tank; tipped up on one side. It had smashed into a partly demolished wall, and rubble almost buried a body that hung half in and half out of the tank like a broken puppet. In that heart-stopping moment before realisation set in, the blood drained from Vadek's face and his pupils dilated. The shock knocked him breathless, and for several seconds he was unable to absorb what he was seeing; for the truth was too terrible to bear. His beloved cousin, his best friend, was dead.

This, then, was the grim reality of war. Not someone giving orders from a desk in the safety of their office, hoping the end would justify the means, but the death of a loved one, fighting for a cause he passionately believed in and having to kill or be killed. The reality of war was death, and it was staring him in the face.

As he stood there, his face devoid of colour, not moving, staring, just staring, the inane thought came to him that it was 19 May. It was his birthday, and he was twenty-five years old.

THIRTEEN

ITALY, MAY–JULY 1944

WE ARE COMRADES IN LIFE AND DEATH. WE SHALL
CONQUER TOGETHER, OR WE SHALL DIE TOGETHER.

WINSTON CHURCHILL TO GENERAL
SIKORSKI, 18 JUNE 1940

The battle for Monte Cassino was the bloodiest of the war, but the fighting was not over. The heavily fortified town of Piedimonte was part of the second stage of the Cassino assault, and the exhausted, depleted Polish troops had been ordered to take it. So Vadek was on the move again with the rest of his unit; bodies weary, faces glistening in the rain as they pushed on under leaden skies. But for Vadek, it did not matter. Nothing mattered any more.

The fighting and combat continued for several days as the troops, barely recovered from the terrible slaughter of Monte Cassino, fought to take Piedimonte. The Germans had turned the town into a fortress surrounded by extensive minefields. Every day was a hard-fought struggle against the onslaught of machine-gun fire and shelling. Undaunted, the Polish artillery pummelled the town into rubble until on 24 May, after five days of continuous and bitter fighting, the battle-weary Poles finally captured Piedimonte.

Vadek had little time to grieve, though the trauma of Monte Cassino and the death of his beloved cousin Andrzei affected him deeply. The images constantly played before his eyes, but he had to push them to the very deepest recesses of his subconscious. For he was in the middle of a war and only when it was over could he finally mourn his cousin. But at night Vadek remembered and would wake up shouting, shaking and bathed in sweat as the horrors of what he had witnessed came back to haunt him.

Still the men marched onward, in appalling weather, doggedly pushing north towards the seaport of Ancona through quagmires sown with mines.

Heavy army boots slithered in the boggy, uneven ground as the men staggered onwards. And always there was the rain; continuous driving rain, mercilessly beating down as Italy experienced its worst weather for many years. Vadek could not remember the last day he had seen any sunshine. The persistent damp weather with its gloomy grey skies made everyone feel miserable and wretched.

On 16 June, General Anders had issued the order: 'Pursue the enemy at the highest possible speed and capture Ancona harbour.'

Ancona, three hundred and fifty miles from Piedimonte, was close to the fighting; its capture would enable the Allies to shorten their lines of communication. To reach the city, the Second Polish Corps had to cross the heavily defended Chienti river They reached it on 21 June, but heavy fighting continued in the area for almost ten more days. As the Poles gradually pushed forward the Germans fell back.

Vadek's mind shut itself off from the carnage all around him. As bloody fighting followed yet more bloody fighting, as friends and allies were blown up in front of his shell-shocked eyes, he mechanically did the job he was trained for; firing shells, loading and reloading, blasting the enemy, closing his heart and his mind and blocking out the screams of the wounded and dying .

Along with other allied forces the Polish artillery bombarded the area with a non-stop barrage of shells. On the morning of 17 July, the Poles secured Monte della Crescia, and that same evening took Casenuove, outflanking the German troops, while the British Eighth Army secured Montecolle and Croce di San Vincenzo. The following day, with no time to rest, the Polish infantry took the stronghold of Offagna, nine miles from Ancona, while their armoured divisions succeeded in reaching the sea, effectively cutting off the Germans from the north-west. After just over a month of bloody fighting, and taking other smaller strongholds surrounding the city, the Poles pushed the German infantry back over the river and, jubilant, captured Ancona on 18 July.

The capture of the town and its harbour, enabling the faster delivery of essential supplies to the Allied forces along the Adriatic coast, was the only operation totally planned and carried out by the Polish armed forces, as a separate force.

During that seemingly endless summer of continuous fighting, the tide of war was turning against the Germans, and Hitler was now facing opposition on two fronts, with the Allied forces moving across northern France and the Red Army closing in from the east.

Over the years, many prominent German army officers had become dis-illusioned with Hitler's leadership and they now wanted to bring the war to an end. As a consequence, on 20 July at the Wolf's Lair in East Prussia, several German military leaders, including Rommel, attempted to assassinate Hitler.

But the bomb, planted by Colonel Claus Schenk von Stauffenberg, gave Hitler only minor injuries; it had been hidden in a briefcase put down against a table leg, but Hitler had moved away at the crucial moment. Stauffenberg, who had served with Rommel in the Afrika Korps, was executed by firing squad the next day. Other officers were hung with piano wire from meat hooks and suffered a slow, agonising death. On 14 October, Rommel was, due to his rank and his status as a national hero, given the option of suicide, thereby sparing his family. He chose the cyanide pill.

This attempt was one of several that had gone before, and prompted the head of the German press to write that the failure to take the life of the German leader was a sign of divine intervention Hitler himself believed that he had been saved to continue with his work.

Meanwhile, Vadek still was a long way from his beloved homeland, and preparations had already begun for the next advance, Operation Olive. The Second Polish Army Corps was charged with the breaking the Gothic Line. This was the last major line of defence in Italy; it ran along the northern Apennines, a series of mountain ranges that form the backbone of Italy. After the fall of Rome, the German forces had withdrawn to this line, a string of heavily fortified positions north of Florence, blocking the route north to Austria.

So there was to be no respite for the battle-weary Polish troops as they pressed on yet again. Continually pushing north, forcing the German forces back as they advanced towards Pesaro, on the Adriatic coast thirty-five miles or so north of Ancona.

They ate while on the march, sitting wherever a rock could be found, for the ground was always soggy and the trees dripping. They carried a few tins of food in their rucksacks as often there was no time or place to set up a kitchen tent. These tins usually contained sardines, corned beef, or bully beef as the Brits called it, and Spam. They loved their Spam, Vadek came to realise, though the tasteless pork mush was not something he was familiar with. There were tinned peaches, condensed milk and small packets of hard, dry biscuits which were not very appetising or sweet, but full of vitamins. Vadek was not too fond of the biscuits – they made him cough – but they were bearable if dipped in tea. He thought it bizarre that the British put the sweet, sticky condensed milk into their tea, which he always had black, and he frequently swapped his milk for another soldier's peaches.

Meanwhile, the First Polish Armoured Division landed in Normandy on 1 August as part of the First Canadian Army detachment. Unbeknownst to them at the time – and indeed to all the Poles fighting in Europe – that date would forever be remembered in Polish history. For that was the day when the people of Warsaw rose up in arms against their German oppressors and began their fight for freedom.

Though their country had been occupied for years, the citizens of Poland had never given up the fight for the freedom of their country. At the outset of war they had formed a resistance movement which later become known as the Armia Krajowa – the Home Army – with the aim of freeing their capital city and beginning a general uprising when the time was right.

Now it was midsummer and Soviet tank patrols had been seen on the outskirts of the city, on the far bank of the Vistula. Surely now the time was ripe for the revolt. Though the Poles knew they were outnumbered and had barely enough supplies and weapons to last a week, with a policy of 'one bullet one German' and Russian tanks ready to come to their aid, surely they could not lose!

General Tadeusz Komorowski, commander of the Polish Underground and better known by his code name Bór, 'forest', was an accomplished rider who had fought with the cavalry in the Russian/Polish war of 1919.

He set the date for 1 August. At 5 pm that sultry summer evening, a bomb blasted the Nazi headquarters in Warsaw and the Polish Underground surged out from the sewers into the streets, flinging themselves onto any German they saw, with weapons or tools, or bits of wood, whatever they could find, even their bare hands. The Germans were taken by surprise but quickly counter-attacked, and with their tiger tanks, pushed their way through the city to the banks of the Vistula.

On the far side were the Russians – now an ally of Poland and watching everything from the safety of the river – but they did nothing to help, obeying Stalin's orders not to intervene and to retreat. This was because Stalin was planning on taking control of the city once the war was over and he did not want the Poles to make it a stronghold.

So the Poles were abandoned, the Russian leader even refusing to let Allied planes use airfields in Soviet-held territory to drop supplies to the desperate Polish people.

The Underground radio called for all Poles everywhere to join in the fight for freedom, and so the civilians rallied to their capital's defence, joining the resistance and the Underground fighters. Paving slabs were pulled up and hurled at the tanks, young children threw stones and rocks at German soldiers and schoolchildren carried messages from one group to another, then disappeared into the maze of sewers under the city streets. Everywhere could be seen the painted symbol of the Polish Underground, the inspiring *kotwica* (anchor) incorporating the letters P and W (*Polska Walcząca*, Fighting Poland) .

The Germans had been ordered to kill every Pole, young or old. Daily there were executions, people were hung publicly in the streets, left hanging there for all to see, and no one was allowed to cut them down. Others were lined up against a wall and shot. Men, women, children, the old and the sick, all were executed. No one was to be spared.

Much of Warsaw had been destroyed, the old buildings collapsing like a house of cards, burying many of those who had sought refuge in the cellars. But seemingly miraculously, although the Church of the Holy Cross, housing the heart of Frederic Chopin in one of its pillars, was burnt out, its roof and towers flattened, the pillar and the heart remained untouched.

Across the road from the church was the German headquarters, a formidable stone building with concrete pillars flanking the large double doors. This was the most feared address in Poland, for it was the headquarters of the Gestapo and a brutal interrogation centre. Few, if any, who entered unwillingly came out alive.

The doors opened into a bare corridor, dimly lit with doors to each side leading to cells and interrogation rooms. At the far end was a narrow, windowless room with rows of wooden benches, each facing the same way, towards a bare stone wall. The layout resembled that of a tram; this was the room where prisoners were held prior to interrogation by the dreaded Gestapo, and it instilled a sense of fear into any person who found themselves waiting there. And it could be a wait of several hours, or even days. During this time no prisoner was allowed to eat or sleep, but had to sit still, facing the blood-spattered wall, pockmarked with bullet holes, knowing it was certain death to move.

A guard paced the back of the room behind the benches. Not seen, but heard. To sit there, every sense alert, unable to look. Yet too frightened to look even if one could. It was impossible for any prisoner not to feel the fear generated in that room. The hairs on the back of the neck would rise, palms become clammy, beads of sweat form along the brow. Those footsteps continuously pacing back and forth, back and forth, instilling terror into the very heart and mind of all those who sat there awaiting their fate, knowing they could be sent to the notorious Pawiak prison for execution. But death was the easy way out. Before that was something far worse.

There for all to see were several shelves running along the length of the shorter wall, and it was impossible to turn the eyes away for they were drawn like a magnet to those shelves. There was nothing worse than the knowing ... knowing what they were going to do. Before they came for you, you would be a quivering nervous wreck, far easier to break. For on those shelves, prominently displayed, were the implements of torture; bullwhips, manacles, pliers and more. Even the bravest of men became weak. And everyone talked sooner or later.

A solitary figure sat motionless in the room. The guards had locked the door and left to join the fighting. They were far too distracted by the chaos and confusion all around, to be concerned with just the one prisoner. So Czeslav Kossakowski was alone, but his whole body tensed in anticipation of the return of a guard. He could not see anything of what was happening and though aware of what was going on, was unable to escape. Locked in, he could only sit and wait in helpless fear, alone in the concrete cell.

He had no idea how long he had been there, for every torturous minute stretched into eternity. His nerves were on a knife-edge, and his whole body was taut, expecting at any moment the door of the collective cell to be pushed open by an SS guard. Weak from lack of food, and water, he was disorientated.

He remembered the day he had been taken prisoner following a bungled attempt to derail a German munitions train. With other members of the resistance he had set grenades and explosives along the track, but they had been surprised by a German patrol car. Rapid shooting had ensued and as he had tried to make his escape, he had tripped over a tree root, wrenching his ankle. Frantically, he had told the others who came to his aid to leave him, to go back to the shelter of the woods, for he would only hinder their escape.

Hiding behind a tree, he had fired several rounds at the Germans as they advanced through the trees, shooting as many as he could before being overcome. A rifle butt viciously crashed down onto his injured ankle. A bolt of pain exploded through him and a mist clouded his vision as a wave of unconsciousness swept over him. Dragged into a car, he had regained consciousness in a bare cell and had known immediately where he was. Where all like him were taken: Al Szucha 25. Gestapo headquarters.

For several days he had languished in a filthy, bug-infested cell, with his swollen ankle black and throbbing, forced to listen to the terrible sounds of the blows and thuds from nearby cells. He had covered his ears, desperately trying to block out the awful screams, but he could not. He knew that their fate was his fate, and he suffered the agonies of a fellow Pole – a comrade who was dying so Poland could live.

When would it be his turn? The sounds of those wretched souls was so distressing that he thought he would go mad. The sobs and whimpers of the women pleading, begging for the torment to stop before another high-pitched scream would pierce the air. Then silence. A deadly silence. Then sometimes the whimpering would start again. Never-ending, on and on, and it was all he could do not to shout at them to stop. To finish it. To stop, please stop. For how could anyone make another suffer so? He could not bear to listen.

Then the sheer terror when his cell door had opened and he had been dragged along the corridor, almost passing out with the pain from his ankle, and thrown into the collective cell. To wait.

Now with the guard gone, Czeslav paced up and down despite the pain of his ankle, unable to sit still for more than a few seconds. His nerves were at breaking point, the fear of knowing what they were going to do to him compounded by the sight of the terrible, bloodied instruments of torture. He wanted to be brave and believe he would not say anything, but it was impossible to know how much he could endure before begging for mercy. For beg he surely would. There was little he could tell them, as information was kept to the bare minimum – but he knew it would make no difference. They enjoyed inflicting pain and watching another suffer; it was something the sadistic Gestapo relished and they wouldn't want to be robbed of their entertainment.

As he paced, thoughts whirled around crazily in his head. I'm just a family man, a simple farmer, I just want to go home to my lovely wife. My family. His eyes blurred. *They* are why you are doing this, he told himself firmly. So one day you can be together again. You'll take whatever is coming to you for *them*.

His mind in turmoil, he tried to think positively and clasped the little silver cross around his neck, a present from his wife on their first anniversary. If only he wasn't shut in this awful place, if only he could get out and do something. Far better to be out there fighting than kept here waiting for what must surely come; in a sudden surge of frustration borne out of desperation for his predicament, he hit the wall with his clenched fist.

As he leant against the stone wall, head bent in despair and oblivious to the pain and the blood trickling through his fingers from his knuckles, he stiffened. There were words scrawled on the bare wall. A name caught his eye, Konrad, and the *kotwica*. As he looked more closely he noticed there were other names, and more writing; untidy, uneven words. His pain and fear momentarily forgotten, his sticky fingers traced the words as he read them out loud, his voice echoing eerily in that silent room:

'It is easy to speak about Poland
It is harder to work for her,
Even harder to die for her
and the hardest to suffer for her.'

Czeslav stood upright, feeling ashamed of his own weakness. What poor soul had written this while waiting here in this cell to be tortured? There was no name, no date. It could have been yesterday, last week, last month. What had happened to that brave person? And as he stood there, the tears began to fall. Not for him, not because he was frightened for himself, but for the unknown person who had stood up to the brutality and horror around him.

And Czeslav cried for Poland, for the country he loved so much and would die for, if he had to, as so many had, and so many more would.

The sudden rattle of keys in the lock shattered the silence. He froze, breaking into a cold sweat. Swallowing nervously, with pounding heart he braced himself for what must surely come. In the awful eternity of a single moment he waited, his eyes fixed on the lock … and almost collapsed.

'Pavel! Pavel!' Disbelievingly, weak with immeasurable relief, he could barely speak as they embraced warmly, but in haste. To see not just a Polish face, but the face of his own beloved nephew, was truly astonishing, and his weakened, pain-racked body and mind had difficulty accepting what he was seeing.

'We must hurry; there's not a moment to lose. I knew they'd bring you here – it's where they bring everyone,' said Pavel.

As they hurried through the maze of corridors, Czeslav was sickened by the many corpses littering the building, yet could not help but be grateful that he had escaped the same fate. Reaching an open courtyard at the back end of the building, he realised it was late evening and darkness was fast approaching. The air was thick with dust from the piles of rubble from the blown-up buildings which filled the streets of the once beautiful city. Down a narrow side street, crouching behind the ruins of a wall, they stopped for a moment.

'We must split up. It's too dangerous to stay together; I'm too slow,' Czeslav looked down at his ankle.

Pavel followed his gaze and grimaced, realizing how much of an effort it must have been for his uncle to run.

'No, you won't get far on that; it'll be suicide.' Pavel peered round the edge of the wall. 'These streets are mostly deserted now; the Germans are focusing on the other districts. I know an area that's still in the hands of the resistance, where your ankle can be treated and we can rest a while.'

Looking closely at his uncle's face, gaunt and filmed with sweat, he added, 'It's not too far … if you think you can make it?'

Czeslav nodded silently.

'Good. Let's go – but stay close.' Pavel turned and, crouching low, entered a gloomy street covered with rubble, his uncle following closely behind. It was impossible not to tread on the corpses scattered in the streets; they had been decaying quickly in the heat of the day and were covered with flies. Warsaw was on fire, and the red glow outlined the buildings and lit the sky to the west where clouds of smoke rose over the burning city and embers fell like rain.

Machine-gun fire with spasmodic single shots followed by loud shouting could be heard as the Germans banged loudly on doors, forcing the frightened occupants outside. Keeping low, Czeslav and Pavel watched helplessly as a man, bloodied and beaten, was dragged into the street by two soldiers. Bottles of petrol were thrown into houses that were still occupied and there was no chance of escape for any inside, and the air was filled with the smell of burning bodies.

It was difficult to make their way through the streets, blocked as they were with rubble and barbed wire from broken barricades. Everywhere lay corpses – women with babies, children, pregnant women, half-buried in bricks and debris.

Turning into a narrow side street and scrambling over the bricks and stones, Pavel knelt on the ground searching for a manhole cover.

'I know it's here somewhere,' he said, scrabbling at the bricks while trying to keep as quiet as possible for fear of attracting attention. Together they clawed at the debris, uncaring of their bleeding hands. Minutes passed before a relieved Pavel found the manhole and dragged the cover aside.

The sewers were narrow and gloomy, and the men were forced to crawl along on hands and knees in the filthy water, ever fearful of a grenade or gas canister, or even a surge of electricity. For some time there seemed to be no way out, but at last Pavel stopped, reached up and began to climb up some iron rungs.

Czeslav watched and waited anxiously, for what might have been safe before might not be so now, and Pavel would be in danger if there were any German soldiers nearby. Breathing heavily and pushing hard against the manhole cover, Pavel slowly lifted it up a little and looked through the slit he'd made.

'It's safe,' he said in a voice barely above a whisper.

Pulling himself up and over the top, he was gone, only to reappear a few seconds later, his face glowing eerily in the moonlight as he looked down on his uncle with a reassuring smile. 'Come on.'

Czeslav climbed awkwardly up the ladder, every step an agonising effort. By the time he reached the opening his face was a mask of pain, and he nearly fell as Pavel pulled him through and over the top.

'Almost there,' Pavel said as, in a daze, Czeslav followed almost blindly behind, concentrating on staying close to his nephew despite the waves of pain that washed over him.

At a deserted tenement house that was practically an empty shell with one side open to the elements, Pavel rapped sharply on the door twice, paused, then again twice more. They waited several minutes before it was opened slowly by a slender young woman holding a candle. On seeing Pavel, her face softened into a relieved and welcoming smile. Entering the dismal hallway they continued through several passageways which led into adjoining empty houses. Then they followed her down several stone steps into an empty cellar, the flickering flame throwing eerie shadows around the room and illuminating a large, solid bookcase against the far wall.

'Here, take it,' she said giving the candle to Czeslav and pushing against one side of the bookcase, Pavel lent his weight and as it slowly scraped across the stone floor, Czeslav saw there was a door behind it. The girl knocked twice and a few minutes passed in silence before it opened. Pale light filled the doorway as they filed through. Czeslav watched as the false back of the bookcase was removed, enabling Pavel to drag it back into position in front of the door using the shelves as leverage before replacing the false back. No one spoke as they moved slowly along the passageway, Pavel supporting his uncle who was grunting with pain. The girl stopped and turned to him, telling him sympathetically that they were almost there, and giving a quick look of concern to Pavel as they walked on, to knock at yet another door. This was opened almost immediately, and they stepped forward into a large room housing a kitchen where several members of the Polish Underground had congregated; a far door led to four other rooms, two of which served as a hospital.

Pavel and Czeslav greeted the others, but no names were mentioned. It was safer that way, for who knew what anyone would reveal under torture?

All the beds were occupied except in the cellars. Almost passing out, Czeslav was half-carried down to a bed, and he lay on it breathing heavily from the exertion. Bringing some water for his uncle, Pavel then left saying he would be back shortly. An elderly man who introduced himself as the doctor passed him on the stairs, and they spoke for a few minutes before continuing on their way.

'It's broken, I'm afraid,' said the doctor to Czeslav on examination, 'but I'll do the best I can with what little I have.'

Czeslav winced and gritted his teeth as the doctor held his ankle firmly. 'This will hurt, I'm afraid, but it'll be quick,' and even before he had finished the sentence, with a sudden sharp pull he set the ankle as Czeslav choked back a scream of pain. Beads of sweat lined his forehead as the doctor wrapped a torn piece of sheet securely round his discoloured, swollen ankle, and Czeslav lay back wearily against the mattress, his face pale.

'Rest while you can,' the doctor advised, and left the room with a nod. Pavel returned to his uncle with a welcome cup of hot soup and some bread.

'Supplies are low,' he said, pulling up a chair. 'Soon there'll be nothing left; many parts of the city are already on lower rations than here.' He sighed. 'No one expected it to go on this long. How long can we hold out with no supplies?'

His voice became angry with frustration. 'Why are the Russians just sitting there, watching and waiting like vultures for the final kill. Is there no one we can trust?'

They sat in silence for a few moments, each lost in his own thoughts, and pondering the outcome.

'What of Andrzei … and Vadek? Any news?' asked Czeslav weakly, but with hope in his eyes. 'It's been so long – any news at all? There must be something.'

Pavel looked sadly into his uncle's face, wanting to give him some good news, but he could not. 'I'm sorry. Of Vadek I know nothing.' He paused, then continued. 'He may be a prisoner somewhere … or fighting with the army in Europe. The Allies have landed in Normandy, and surely the war must be over soon, but reliable news is hard to come by.'

Czeslav sighed deeply and sadly, a long drawn-out sigh deep from within his soul.

'There's not a day I don't think of him. But he's strong; I know he'll make it.' He paused, thinking of the son he had not seen or heard anything of for five years.

In a voice full of regret, he added, more to himself than to Pavel. 'I didn't even say goodbye.' And tears welled in eyes clouded with unhappiness.

He stared blankly into his soup then shook his head fiercely as if to dispel any morbid thoughts. 'But what of Andrzei? I've not forgotten your brother. Are his whereabouts known?'

Pavel was relieved he could at least give some news of his brother. 'The last I heard was that Andrzei was with the tank regiment, but where I don't know. Most likely Italy.'

Czeslav put a comforting hand on his nephew's shoulder: 'For that at least we must be thankful. Let's hope and pray they are both alive and safe and having a better time of it than we are.'

He paused then said slowly. 'I haven't thanked you for saving my life. If they'd got to me first …' he paused again and, looking his nephew directly in the eyes, continued, 'I don't know what I'd have done, how long I could have held out … those terrible screams …'

Pavel laid a hand gently on his uncle's arm. 'None of us are brave. We all do what we have to do, and no one knows what that is until the time comes.' Then, almost as an afterthought, 'Bravery isn't an absence of fear, but a consequence of something we have to do.' He paused. 'We're all afraid.'

A tap at the door, and the woman who had led them to the refuge stood there rather shyly, smiling.

'Olivia, come in,' Pavel said warmly, and walked across the room to greet her. He took her hand and smoothed her hair while looking tenderly into her face, which was turned up to his with a happy glow. They spoke quietly for a few seconds before he turned to his uncle and introduced Olivia to him. Czeslav acknowledged her warmly, and watched as they left the room together.

There's something going on there, he thought, smiling to himself as he drifted into an exhausted sleep.

For two more days they stayed in the comparative safety of the hospital, an oasis of calm in a storm. Pavel would disappear during the day, sometimes alone, usually with several others, returning at night with news of what was happening in the city districts and stories of the atrocities committed by the Germans.

The massacre of many thousands of civilians in the Wola district had been intended to crush the will of the people – but instead it strengthened their resolve, as every day more wounded were brought in to the small hospital. It was becoming desperately overcrowded, many wounded having to lie on the floor, even in the cellars, and despite Czeslav's broken foot he and Pavel knew the time had come for them to leave.

The last embers of the dying sun tinged the clouds red, highlighting the city's destruction as Czeslav and Pavel parted company. Clasping one another warmly they faced one another, filled with the knowledge they were risking their lives; the future for both was full of was uncertainty.

'Good luck,' Pavel whispered.

'We'll meet again,' Czeslav said, as much to convince himself as his nephew. 'One day we'll all be back together. You, me, Andrzei, Vadek.'

Pavel nodded, desperately wanting to believe it. Looking around at the panorama of destruction, his gaze lingered on the columns of smoke rising above the ruins into the haze of smoke and dust. The hot dry winds carried the smell of rotting bodies and burnt-out houses into every nook and cranny. Warsaw was dying a cruel and lingering death.

'Life used to be so good,' Pavel's eyes glistened with unshed tears. 'Why did things have to change? What did we do to deserve this?' He brushed away a tear before it could fall.

'And it will be again,' said Czeslav, gripping Pavel's arms. 'You'll see, we'll get it back. We have to. We can't give up – we can't! We had a life worth living for, worth fighting for. And we will again.'

Pavel looked sorrowfully at his uncle. 'Worth dying for?'

Czeslav stared into the dull eyes of his nephew. 'Yes, if we have to,' he said quietly.

They stood there silently, Pavel loath to leave his uncle and Czeslav deeply concerned for his nephew.

'Pavel,' he said, 'take your happiness while you can, for you never know when it will be snatched away from you and lost forever.'

Pavel looked at him, unsure for a second what he had meant, then realisation flickered across his features, and he smiled slowly and nodded.

There was nothing more to say and they both knew what had to be done. They embraced each other desperately, clasping one another tightly.

'Take care of that girl of yours,' Czeslav said with a smile that didn't quite reach his eyes. Then turning abruptly away, he hobbled along the bombed-out street, towards the figure of a member of the resistance almost hidden in the entrance of a dark alley. Together they melted into the shadows, leaving Pavel to gaze sadly after the only member of his family he knew for certain was still alive. Then he too disappeared silently into the maze of broken streets and burned-out houses.

Long harrowing days became even longer weeks, but the citizens of Warsaw held out, even though they were hopelessly outnumbered and had little ammunition or supplies. Every scrap of food had been eaten, and even dogs and rodents killed and consumed; but the brewery remained in their control and so they lived on the barley from its warehouses, grinding and soaking it to make *plij-zupa*, a thick soup.

Self-appointed teams distributed it around the ruined city to the starving people every day, despite the risk of being killed on the spot. Every day was a desperate ordeal, scurrying, rodent-like, from hole to hole along the sewers, and every Pole carried a mental map of the system's layout and escape routes.

It was daybreak and the pale turquoise sky held the promise of another hot, dry day. Pavel was on the run. Droplets of sweat ran down his thin, grimy face. He was weak with hunger and desperately thirsty; the Germans had turned off the water supply weeks earlier. Pausing, he leaned against the rubble of a bombed-out house, his body bent almost double as he fought for breath, his heart pounding.

He had been with a group of distributors. Climbing through the broken window of a derelict house in the search for food, they had been spotted by a passing patrol, and had scattered to evade the Nazi bullets.

Now he sank weakly to the floor, stretching his legs out in front of him. If only he could make it to the nearest sewer he would be safe, but the Germans were getting smarter. They knew the people were using them as escape tunnels and would often be covering the entrances with their flame throwers. He must be constantly on his guard, for the city was teeming with Germans – but for now at least it seemed as though he had evaded the soldiers.

Gingerly, he pushed aside the torn, blood-soaked fabric of his trousers, grimacing as he stared at the gaping hole in his leg. Glancing back along the street, he could see the trail of blood he had left. He must move, and quickly. The sound of steel-capped boots on stone spurred him into action. He knew there was a sewer nearby if only he could find it. Fighting off the waves of dizziness that washed over him, he tore his tattered shirt into a makeshift bandage, hampered by his withered hand, a present from a soldier with a flame-thrower; days earlier he had dropped into a tunnel and pulled the cover shut, but too late.

He winced and gritted his teeth as he wound the bandage tightly round his leg to stem the flow of blood. Then bracing himself, he pulled himself up against the brick wall and staggered along the alleyway, dragging his useless leg behind him.

Barely fifty yards on and he stopped, his face a mask of pain and every nerve alert as the sound of excited German voices told him that they had already found his resting place. There was no time to lose. He hobbled on, cursing his wounded leg. A command rang out: 'Halt, or I fire!!' He paused, then nipped into an alley but at the far end of it was a barricade. It was one that had been constructed by the Poles to prevent tanks entering the city. How foolish of him! With a sinking heart he knew there was no way out. He was cornered. Like a rat in a trap.

He leaned back against a wall and closed his eyes. This was the end. He was not afraid. It was only when he was waiting in his quarters, with time to think, that he would shake; and he was frightened, not just for himself but for others too. Every day, fewer returned – and Olivia, he had not seen Olivia for several days.

Surrounded by the dust and debris of a ruined city, with death and destruction everywhere about him, for a brief moment, his thoughts turned to the lazy days in Kapice. He could almost smell the new-mown hay and touch the sunflowers waving in the breeze.

He thought fondly of his little brother Andrzei. So eager to go to war, always so impulsive, with such a love of life. What of him, where was he now? And his cousin Vadek? So studious, and far too clever! He smiled faintly, sadly; so much had happened. It seemed like a lifetime away. Was it really just a few summers ago they had all been together – Tadek, Henja, and his uncle. Had Czeslav made it to safety, to the forests? He fervently hoped so.

Surely it could not all be for nothing. He would not let it all be for nothing. He thought of Olivia – so little time together, but she had said yes. Yes, of course she would be his wife, and they had laughed and kissed and celebrated with the others. And he smiled at the memory, for they had brought joy into the hearts of others who had been devoid of it for so long.

Please God, please let her stay safe. Let them all be safe.

A half-forgotten line from a bible came unbidden into his mind: 'Grass withers, flowers fall, but the spirit lives on.' And he knew without a shadow of doubt that the spirit of Poland would live on. It would never die while one single Pole remained alive. A small light flickered again in his dull, pain-glazed eyes. His mind was drifting. Weak and light-headed from loss of blood he knew there were only a few seconds left.

The footsteps of the enemy broke into his thoughts; Pavel knew he had one more ace up his sleeve. Slowly, he reached his bloodied fingers into the front pocket of his ripped shirt …

The Germans rounded the corner and stopped in their tracks on seeing him. Quietly sitting there, not moving, head bowed, was he already dead?. They hoped not, or it would spoil their fun.

'No escape for you, then,' they jeered. 'We've got you now, you filthy Polish scum,' and levelled their rifles. Pavel raised his arm and threw his last grenade: 'For Poland!' he shouted defiantly, 'and victory!'

After sixty-three days of bitter fighting over 200,000 Poles had lost their lives. On 2 October 1944, Bór surrendered to the German command

A week after the surrender Himmler gave the order to destroy what was left of Warsaw brick by brick. Any buildings left standing in the city were blown up, and the once beautiful city was systematically razed to the ground. Nearly all citizens left alive were sent to German prisons or death camps. Resistance leaders were shot, often after the most terrible torture.

But a few of them had fled into the forests to join other partisans to fight again for their homeland, even though their commander, General Tadeusz 'Bór' Komorowski, was sent to the maximum security prison of Colditz, in eastern Germany.

FOURTEEN

ITALY, SPRING 1945

THE POLISH NATION'S SUFFERINGS HAVE NOT BEEN ABATED AND FOR US, FAITHFUL POLISH SOLDIERS, THE TIME TO RETURN TO OUR COUNTRY HAS NOT YET COME.

GENERAL ANDERS, ITALY, 1 SEPTEMBER 1946

Rumours had been flying around for weeks and there was an air of expectancy.

Vadek had not been home for six years, nor heard any news from his family. He was weary of the fighting and of never staying in more than one place for more than a few months at a time. He had blanked his mind from the horrors, the blood, the carnage. His friends, wounded, dying. Dead. So many gone. It was as if he too were dead. He didn't know if he would ever feel anything again. He didn't want to feel; to remember. It hurt too much. Far more than any physical pain.

He didn't know whether his mother was alive. If any of his family were still alive. And Ana; what of her, where was she? He could still picture her face as clearly as if it were yesterday, with her eyes that lit up whenever she saw him. He dared not think of what might have happened to her. To any of them. He desperately hoped to return home to Poland. It was this burning hope that had kept him alive through all the horrors he had witnessed and the suffering he had endured.

The wind of change was blowing through Europe and Germany was on the defensive as Russian troops were now approaching Berlin. There was news almost daily of another battle won and another town liberated. But none of this had any impact on Vadek.

In January 1945, the Polish Corps had reached the Senio river, but had ground to a halt. The ground was sodden, making armoured operations impossible. The only other route across the river was through its upper reaches – but there the terrain was rough and jagged with sharp peaks and near-vertical slopes; even a mule could barely negotiate the hairpin bends and steep descents. January marked the start of three months of preparation for the assault on Bologna.

In February, General McCreery, the new British commander of the Eighth Army, met General Anders to discuss the situation and the plan of action. It was during this meeting that Anders learnt of the Allied plan for Poland; it was to be handed over to the Russian Communist regime to be a satellite state of the Soviet Union. He had always expected this but had refused to believe it, hoping that the British and the United States would never allow such a thing to happen, but the news confirmed his worst fears. It was the ultimate betrayal. How could he tell his men? His men who had given so much, suffered so much and endured so much for so long, driven ever onwards by the burning ideal that through their suffering Poland would be free?

How could he ask his men to continue to fight for a country that would no longer be theirs? To die for a country that would no longer be their home? To live in a country they would have no control over? No rights, no voice. It would be a shattering blow.

But when he heard that there were no other reserves, General Anders, having thought for a moment, affirmed that his men would do their duty; whatever the cost, Hitler had to be defeated.

Bombing and bombardment of the German positions on the Senio began in the early morning of 9 April. American and British forces engaged the German flanks while the Poles advanced directly. A wave of Allied bombers missed their target, the friendly fire killing thirty-seven Polish infantry and wounding almost two hundred.

Despite stiff resistance, the Poles took control of the river and set up a bridgehead. During the next few days other Polish divisions, trudging under fire through muddy minefields – some German, some British – took control of further sectors.

Control of the river led to the capture of Imola on 15 April by the Polish troops from their old enemy the German paratroopers, whose flag was given to General Anders. Now for Bologna! The Allies could forget the precipitous tracks, and use the road to transport supplies, arms and troops.

Bologna was a key communication point and a pivotal part of the Allied spring offensive. From his position on its outskirts, Vadek fired his guns on the town for twelve days, covering his colleagues and forcing the Germans to retreat. It was in the early hours of 21 April that the last detachment of Germans fled the town.

So it was that the Poles had secured the city by dawn; the rays of the rising sun fell on the Polish flag as it was hoisted over the magistrate's office. Polish soldiers and tanks were covered with flowers thrown by the excited townspeople as they marched triumphantly, followed by the American troops who had joined them, through the crowded streets, with cries of '*Viva Polonia!*' ringing in their ears,

Vadek felt happy; happiness was an emotion he had not experienced for such a long time that he had almost forgotten there was such a thing. He felt a resurgence of hope as he marched through the town, surrounded by jubilant voices and exultant faces. The warm fingers of the early morning sun softly stroked his face, and for the first time in many years he felt free. He *was* free! And it was a truly wonderful feeling. Nothing could take this moment away.

And after so much rain, the grey sky had turned blue. It was a beautiful spring day; and the sun was shining.

The Battle of Bologna was the Second Polish Corps' last major action, though Vadek's unit had been ordered to carry on driving out the many German detachments that remained in the area. The Poles destroyed three more enemy divisions, before being ordered to stand down on 22 April 1945.

The war in Europe was over!

On 28 April, Generaloberst Heinrich von Vietinghoff sent emissaries to the Allied army headquarters, and the next day formally signed the instrument of surrender on behalf of the German armies in Italy. That same day, Mussolini was killed by Italian partisans. However it was not until 2 May that hostilities finally ceased, with the news that Hitler had committed suicide on 30 April, the day the Russians entered Berlin. The Allies accepted Germany's surrender, and on 8 May 1945 Churchill declared the war in Europe to be at an end.

Nearly everyone – Allied or Axis – was hugely relieved. The peoples of the Allied countries were swept along on a tide of euphoria. There was dancing in the streets, bonfires were lit – it was one huge party. People delirious with happiness, laughing and crying at the same time, wanted to hug and kiss anybody and everybody they met. Strangers in the streets, soldiers, officers, they all wanted to express the overwhelming surge of joy and relief that washed over them and be a part of that momentous, wonderful, amazing moment in history that would forever be ingrained in their memory.

But with the euphoria came conflicting emotions and sombre reflection, remembering those who had died, those who had given their lives for this day and the sacrifices that had been made. So many people had lost everything – home, friends, family. For many survivors, the end of hostilities seemed surreal.

For Vadek, too, this was the day he had waited for so long; but he was never able to forget the brutality and the suffering of the labour camp, or the carnage at Monte Cassino. He would relive in nightmares throughout his life the images of what he had witnessed, and often in daytime too. They were imprinted forever in the deepest recesses of his mind.

Mingled with his joy was a deep sadness for his lost friends and his comrades in arms, and especially for Andrzei. All those who had suffered so terribly with him, in the nightmare of the camps and on the bloody battlefields. Why had he, Vadek, survived? For so long he had walked hand in hand with death. How had he survived?

But now at last, after six long years, came the thrilling realisation that he could now fulfil his dream. He could go home.

FIFTEEN

BETRAYAL

Poland had played an active part in the war from the first to the last; and Poland was the heaviest loser on the winning side. Under an agreement with the Allied leaders – but with no consultation whatsoever with the people of Poland or any of the other countries concerned – in February 1945, Stalin, Churchill and Roosevelt had signed the Yalta Agreement.

In fact, it had been in the autumn of 1943 in Tehran that the Western Allies had sealed Poland's fate; at the end of the war, Poland was to be handed over to Soviet rule. The Yalta Agreement served only to confirm this.

(During the Yalta conference Stalin proposed executing 50,000 German officers to prevent Germany starting another war. President Roosevelt, assuming it was a joke, suggested 49,000, at which Churchill stormed out of the meeting. He was only persuaded to come back in by Stalin's disarming statement that of *course* it was a joke.)

And so Poland would groan under the Russian yoke for a further forty-five years. One sadistic dictator had been replaced with another and former Polish soldiers were imprisoned or shot, making it impossible for Vadek to return to his country.

For Poles, now informed of the Yalta decision, the time when others were celebrating victory was a period of uncertainty and disillusionment, and a shattering of the dreams that had sustained them for so long.

On 1 September 1945, six years to the day after Germany had invaded Poland, a consecration ceremony was held at the Polish war cemetery on the hillside of Monte Cassino. Plans for this memorial had been discussed shortly after the battle itself, in the July of that same year. Prominent and

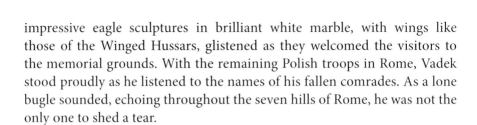

impressive eagle sculptures in brilliant white marble, with wings like those of the Winged Hussars, glistened as they welcomed the visitors to the memorial grounds. With the remaining Polish troops in Rome, Vadek stood proudly as he listened to the names of his fallen comrades. As a lone bugle sounded, echoing throughout the seven hills of Rome, he was not the only one to shed a tear.

AND SO TO ENGLAND, 1946–1947

The Second Polish Corps were still scattered throughout Italy, their headquarters in Ancona. Several units had been assigned to patrol the harbours, airports and railways, for though the war in Europe was over, the Pacific war was still alive.

It had been decided to transfer the Poles to Britain; this had begun in the spring and would continue until late winter that year.

Shamefully, the Polish soldiers who were already in England were not invited to the Victory Day parade; Churchill feared antagonising Stalin, whose help was still needed, now against Japan. Meanwhile, US President Truman, who had replaced Roosevelt after his death, was concerned that Stalin was becoming too powerful and did not want him to invade the Far East. So the decision was taken for a pre-emptive strike; two atom bombs were dropped on Japan.

As a result, on 14 August 1946 Japan surrendered. The war in the Pacific was over. Stalin, pipped at the post, was furious. Thus started the Cold War: two aggressive superpowers who never quite dared use their atomic weapons for fear of destroying themselves.

In 1945, Vadek had enrolled at the University of Rome to continue his studies, and became fluent in Italian with a very good command of English; though his pronunciation often led to some confusion.

He took the time to visit the Coliseum, the Vatican and other great land-marks in the ancient city. Strolling through the Roman amphitheatre, imbued as it was with the echoes of its bloody past, he felt compelled to stop and look around the arena. He could almost hear the ring of steel against steel and the baying of the spectators for blood as they watched a gladiator fighting for his freedom or dying in the attempt. His vision blurred; there in front of him was Andrzei, fired up with enthusiasm – a Winged Hussar riding into battle, a Second World War general, a Roman gladiator – all these were Andrzei.

Vadek never forgot the day he left mainland Europe, his homeland and his family. His was one of the last consignments, departing in February 1947. Basyl had left some months earlier. Fortunately there had been time for them to say their goodbyes to each other; two friends who had endured so much and yet survived, but had lost their homes and their country. Each promised to look for each other in England, but knew not where they would be posted once they arrived there.

First, a train journey to Naples; standing room only, and men jostled for space next to the windows. At the harbour there was a long queue to fill in papers; every man was then given £10 sterling. Now the transition camp; the wait here could be several weeks. However the time in the camp was put to valuable use, with talks and lectures to prepare them for life in England with its very different political system, customs and lifestyle in general.

Not all the Poles travelled by sea from Naples; some divisions travelled to England by train. Vadek was one of these, and he was not sure which he would have preferred given the choice, for trains and ships were equally uncomfortable and overcrowded. But from a train the men could see the devastation of the cities for themselves and the effects the war had had on the countries of Europe. It was a sombre realisation.

On arrival at the port of Le Havre in north-west France, it was another five long drawn-out days of waiting in a crowded camp in dismal weather before the men embarked for Portsmouth.

There was a general belief that this was merely a temporary situation, and that when things improved they would return to their own country. Nonetheless, it was with a choking sense of farewell that the men watched the coast of Europe until it disappeared over the horizon, the winter sun sparkling on the water like a thousand diamonds.

With a heavy heart and a feeling of emptiness, Vadek stood disconsolately, leaving behind his broken dreams, his face catching the breeze as the French coastline receded. Now the men were faced by the dreadful uncertainty of living in a strange country and a strange language; something they had not envisaged when fighting for their homeland. It was a shattering blow, and no one spoke.

Vadek pulled out the photograph he had carried with him for so long. Now tattered and crumpled, the grainy faces of his mother, father and two younger brothers smiled out at him. Not so young now, he thought with a wry smile as he remembered Roman's cheeky face and chubby legs as he followed Vadek around the farm. And Stanislav; he barely knew him he realised sadly. Would he even remember his older brother Vadek?

A sudden gust of wind caught the photograph. Too late he reached out; but it was gone, carried away like a butterfly. There was nothing he could do. Only watch in abject misery, as the one thing he had left of his home and family, which had given him strength in his worst moments, shimmered briefly before falling onto the waves and floating away. Floating back the way they had come; back towards Europe and his homeland.

As they approached the English shore, the Poles stood there silently, watching in apathy. This was not a time for celebration. But the band on the pier struck up as they docked and disembarked, accompanied by cheers from British sailors on neighbouring boats. But there were no welcoming crowds, for no one wanted the Poles there. Vadek felt isolated, and few Poles could raise a smile in response to the sailors. They had lost too much.

Stepping onto the dock, Vadek stopped and stared about him; huge, grey cauliflower clouds tinged with darker grey, hung low in the sky and a fresh breeze blew across the dockyard. Looking about him, he walked towards the convoy waiting to take the new arrivals to their camps. As he stood in line waiting to climb into the truck, the realisation hit him like a hammer blow; all he possessed in the world – everything – was right there with him. Packed in his kit bag.

The largest contingent of troops was sent to camps in industrial areas in the north of England and the Midlands, giving the men a chance of finding work in the factories. Others went to agricultural areas, some in the south, to Scotland. So the men faced another arduous journey by train and lorry to their camps, where they were told to immediately enlist at the nearest Polish Resettlement Camp (PRC). Vadek was billeted at Witley Resettlement Camp in Godalming, Surrey, so had only a short onward journey.

The camps, though basic, were equipped with kitchens, laundry rooms and communal shower cubicles, the beds were in wooden barracks. But many of those buildings had no heating, and the winter of 1946/47 turned out to be the coldest and longest on record. Nevertheless, the public gardens were well kept and tended by the Poles, and Vadek immersed himself in growing turnips, swedes and cabbages. The men were encouraged to participate in sports such as football and rugby, but Vadek had never enjoyed those games and had no intention of starting now. Unfamiliar with cricket, after watching a few matches he decided he wasn't really missing much. He was plagued with pains in his knee; X-rays showed that his leg had fractured some years previously and had reset itself awkwardly. As a result, for the rest of his life it could not support his weight; it was a lasting legacy of his time in Siberia.

There was little time to be idle, for there were classes in English and geography, local politics and of course the complicated British currency. Like so many other Poles, Vadek knew nothing at all or very little about these, but was eager to learn.

Food was not plentiful; England had many shortages – and for the Poles this was unexpected as there had been no such restrictions in Italy. So a ration card came as rather a shock. Throughout 1947 even potatoes were rationed and there was only one egg a fortnight per person; if you were last in line there could be nothing at all. Vadek sometimes found himself having queued for something he had not wanted, when he had not understood what he was waiting for.

One of the few things that weren't rationed, Vadek noted dismally, was boot polish; he was still being paid by the British army, and boots had to be polished to a mirror finish. There was milk, three pints a week; it was in 1946 that free milk had been brought into schools. Bread, though scarce, was not rationed – but after queuing for several hours, Vadek was not impressed with the tasteless pap of the soft white bread. He longed for the substantial and satisfying rye bread he had grown up with.

As long as he had enough potatoes for either dumplings or pancakes, Vadek was unconcerned about those rations, though he had to use them sparingly. But an egg was needed to bind the grated potato, and one egg in fourteen days was never enough. Egg substitute was a vile-tasting, yellow powder that when he tried it out not only did not work but tasted so awful that he spat it out, annoyed at himself for wasting some of his precious potatoes.

The simple task of making pancakes would remind him of home; in fact there was always something that evoked a memory of a life now long gone. So he concentrated on his studies and kept himself occupied with the aim of getting a good job – and one day returning to his homeland.

Unbeknownst to Vadek and the other Poles, who had very little or no information about their loved ones in their homeland, the situation there was dire. With hindsight, though, it may have been better that they did not know, for – as Vadek was to find out many years later – the truth was far more terrible than anything he could ever have imagined, and to have had to live with that knowledge, unable to do anything about it, would have been truly soul-destroying.

Vadek remembered the other times he had been forced to adapt to a change thrust upon him. This time, the language, with its many different dialects, was no doubt the worst hurdle to overcome. But it was not the only problem, for many English people resented food and jobs being taken by foreigners when they had so little themselves. In some areas, there were protest marches with placards: *Poles go home*. All this had a crushing effect on Vadek's compatriots, who had not asked to be there, nor indeed wanted to be. It only served to make them more homesick than they already were.

Regardless, the soldiers had to actively seek work and show proof of doing so, accepting any job offered, however menial. If a job was not found within two years, pay would be stopped and there was the very real threat of being sent back to Poland. So it was not unusual to find someone with technical skills working as a kitchen porter or a cleaner.

Vadek was fortunate, for he was given the chance to enrol at Nottingham Technical College and there he gained a scholarship to further his education, enabling him to continue at Nottingham University under a government scheme to help ex-servicemen. This was quite an achievement, as everything was of course in English.

To encourage the men to integrate with English people, events such as tea dances were organised, and it was here that Vadek met a girl by the name of Kathy who would feature prominently in his life.

On moving out of the camp, most solders preferred familiarity and settled in areas with their colleagues, for with them they could reminisce and converse in their own language, reducing the pressure on them. They had to carry ID cards at all times, to be produced whenever asked for proof of identity.

It was while he was in Nottingham that Vadek found his close friend, Basyl Lesowiec, at the nearby Replacement Camp. For both, this was a wonderful – and highly emotional – moment, for to have found someone they knew, who had been a part of their life in the most dramatic of circumstances and was now the only familiar person in a strange, and in some ways unwelcoming, country, gave them great happiness, and the bond they had for each other was intense.

They decided to rent rooms together; they found some in an old and dingy three-storey house, as did many ex-servicemen; such lodgings were plentiful in the Nottingham area, where hard-pressed families were only too glad to ease their finances by letting out a room or two.

After qualifying in mathematics and gaining the highest diploma in textiles, Vadek found work as a dyer, and in 1950 began employment with W. Lowe Ltd in its Stuart Street works in Derby, a small industrial town some eight miles from Nottingham. With this position he entered mainstream British life.

The workplace was hot from the steam generated by the boiling dye vats. Such a situation certainly was not something he had ever envisaged, but he was proud to have achieved the qualifications necessary and to have a job; a good job which drew on his mathematical skills. Working hard and proving competent, he earned the respect of his co-workers and his employers, working his way up to be a supervisor. Some years later he took the opportunity of becoming the manager of a dyeing department in Bata, East Tilbury, a leading shoe manufacturer. His was a well-paid and highly skilled profession, for at that time there were no computers to calculate the ratio of dyes to fabrics. With so many companies manufacturing the goods so desperately needed after the shortages of war, Vadek had his pick of where to work.

He never forgot Ana. But he had no way of knowing if she had survived the war nor where she was. Communication between the people of Poland and England was not permitted, and his family had no idea of his whereabouts or if he had survived; likewise he did not know if any of his family were still living.

Fortunately, the Bialystok region was one of the few parts of eastern Poland that had not been partitioned and its people displaced. This meant that the Kossakowskis and their neighbours were allowed to remain in their homes. If they had been moved into Germany – as were so many Polish people forced to abandon their homes – it is highly unlikely that Vadek would have ever been able to trace his family, for they had no way of knowing where he was and he would have never been able to trace their whereabouts. However, the fact that Camilla and Czeslav could stay at home was not without its problems, as the Russian people were allowed to move across the border freely, and there was nothing the Kossakowskis could do about the many groups of Russian refugees who camped on the edges of their fields.

Vadek knew nothing of this, but never a day passed without a thought of them. Many things reminded him of Ana, and there were many times he imagined her there with him and the life they could have shared.

But it was not meant to be, and he had to move on. He had to forget.

It was while living in digs with his friend Basyl and several other Polish servicemen, he first met Irene Clarke. She was to become his wife, though their first meeting did not go well. Irene clearly remembered how late one night, when walking home from her shift at a nearby factory, she feared she was being stalked. Behind her for some time had been walking a man wearing a trench coat, the collar turned up high with his cap pulled down over his face and both hands deep inside the pockets, looking, as she put it, 'decidedly shifty'.

On approaching her home, she was reluctant to go into the house in case he waited outside; she did not want him to see which house she entered. So she turned around to face him, shouting loudly at him to stop following her. Vadek in total bewilderment, replied in his very poor English and his strong Polish accent, that this was where he lived, and he pointed to the house directly opposite. However, Irene still did not trust him and threatened to call the police. It was only when he showed her his ID card with address and photograph inside, that she believed him.

A few days later, Basyl and Vadek were at the local tea dance, Kathy came to speak to Vadek and introduced him to her sister … Irene.

Vadek remembered their first date together later in a nearby cinema: 'I couldn't understand her or she me; but she understood the movie so I just sat and held her hand.'

They were married in 1951 and remained together for almost thirty years until her death at age seventy. Vadek insisted on painting his first proper home, where they lived for almost twenty-five years, in the red and white of the Polish flag!

On 28 November 1947, Vadek was officially discharged from the Second Polish Army Corps. Like his compatriots, Vadek was given the option to relocate to other Western countries – the United States, Australia or Canada – or to remain in England. The men who had married Italian women during and after the Italian campaign chose to return to Italy, others to America or Canada – but for Vadek the choice was simple; England was nearer to his homeland.

For many years after the war it was truly a fearful, terrible time to live in Poland. While Vadek was trying to adjust to his new life in England, with all the problems and difficulties that came with it, the people of Poland lived in a state of terror.

Though Stalin had promised free general elections they never happened, and a Russian-controlled Communist government was imposed. Russians were allowed to roam freely across the borders and there was anarchy and lawlessness under what was a puppet government, controlled by a dictator who had no time for or interest in the country he had bargained for, and which was left in the hands of corrupt officials. Any Pole who protested against the government could be shot or just disappeared. This was not the country the Poles had fought so valiantly for and so desperately wanted to return to. So, like many other Polish soldiers, for Vadek there was only the one option: to remain in England.

It has to be noted that, ironically, Stalin, the very man who had imprisoned and condemned Vadek to a life of living hell, was also his saviour, his liberator; for if fate had taken a different path – that is, if the Soviet Union had not been invaded by Germany – it is extremely unlikely that Vadek would have survived.

The years in the gulag took a tremendous toll on Vadek's mind and body, how much more could he, or any of the men have endured; for the two years there had seemed like twenty, and made him old before his time.

As a former prisoner in a Russian gulag, Vadek had some idea what to expect if he were to return to his country; he well remembered the cruelty of the NKVD. Of those who chose to return, many met a tragic fate; Stalin regarded those who had fought against the Red Army as traitors, and former soldiers of the Second Polish Army Corps were treated as such. There were arrests and deportations, and shootings; many were sent to the gulags and left to die there, with no contact at all with their families. Men who had fought bravely under wartime conditions were treated as criminals; this oppression reached a peak in 1951 when there were mass deportations to labour camps in Siberia.

For over a decade, those who lived in Communist Poland were not allowed to associate in any way with veterans of the Polish Army. There was no communication for Vadek's family, who did not know if he was alive or dead – and he, like others in the West, knew that if he tried to write or visit, the repercussions on the families would be horrific.

The secret police were everywhere, even in schools, where no mention of the bravery of the Poles could be made. No one was allowed to talk openly about any aspect of the war that involved the Poles. Nor to mention any member of family who had fought in the war or try to contact them; this was punishable by imprisonment.

Late in 1958, Vadek received his first letter – heavily censored, but it *was* a letter from home. That was the first of the letters and parcels that could now be sent. But all were opened and read, the parcel's contents often being removed. But at last, after almost twenty years, Vadek's mother finally had the news she had never given up hope of receiving. Her son was alive.

But sadly, Vadek never had the chance to see his father again, for though Czeslav survived the war, he died aged eighty-two, at peace on his farm, long before the day when Vadek was able to return without fear of imprisonment.

KAPICE, 1966

When that day came for Vadek, it was not without a certain amount of apprehension, for Poland, still under the Communist regime and part of the Soviet bloc, was not a free country. After a train journey of almost four days, with constant passport checks on the way, he could see that his homeland was within reach. However, at the Polish border there was a wait in an interrogation cell; Soviet officials took his passport and visa, and questioned him as to why he was returning, wanting to know of his activities in England and during the war. This revived his traumatic memories of imprisonment, so many years before, but as if only yesterday; despite his attempts to block them out, they had resurfaced far too often over the years. Now they reared their ugly head once again. Vadek was terrified that he might not be released, and knew that extreme caution was needed in his replies. So it was with a great sense of relief that after several days' detention he passed through border control, to step at long last, after an eternity of waiting, onto Polish soil.

He had expected change, and had prepared himself, but it still came as a shock, for the country had changed dramatically and was now a place he barely recognised. He felt immense sorrow for what had been lost and the suffering his family had been forced to endure over the twenty-one years since the war in Europe had ended.

The towns were devoid of all colour, and grim concrete apartment blocks housed the occupants, all painted in communist grey, for under the collective regime, no one could appear different from their neighbour. Streets were drab, shops had empty shelves, and the food, what little there was, was rationed. Soulless houses with no individuality, no coloured doors, no window boxes nor gardens – for these had no practical use, and the buildings reflected the grey personality of the man who was governed every aspect of life: Stalin, the Man of Steel.

The countryside at least seemed more welcoming, for the fields were well tended; but there was no pride in what was achieved, and people had lost the incentive to work, for a very large percentage of crops were collected by a state official, with only a very small amount of money paid and often none at all. Each farmer had the same size plot and same number of livestock, but farmers were at least permitted to keep a small area around their home to grow some food for themselves.

Vadek was shocked to see so many itinerant Russian people. The problem was that the situation in their own country was dire, and though they were not allowed to camp in their makeshift tents or ramshackle caravans on farms that belonged to Poles, there was nothing anyone could do about them along the borders, on the roadsides and in the forest.

This, then, was the scene that welcomed Vadek on his first return visit to his homeland; but he was home, and after twenty-seven years of waiting he could at last hug his mother. Love and emotion overwhelmed them both.

EPILOGUE

In 1987, **Vadek** was granted an audience with the Polish Pope John Paul in the Vatican City. For his actions at Cassino and Piedimonte, Vadek was awarded several commendations and the Commemorative Cross of Monte Cassino. He twice received the Bronze Cross of Swords for brave deeds and valour in perilous situations, and the Italian Star for bravery in the Italian campaign.

Waclaw 'Vadek' Piotr Kossakowski died peacefully in 2014 aged ninety-five, on the Isle of Wight, England. According to his deathbed request, his ashes were sent to Poland by his daughters, Lynn and myself; he was given a soldier's funeral and was laid to rest in the family plot beside his father, mother and two brothers.

Camilla, who had continued to milk her cow every day at 4 am, died just two weeks before her hundredth birthday.

Ana never gave up hope of seeing Vadek again, but several years after the war, not knowing if he was alive or dead, she married and had a daughter. She remained close to the Kossakowski family, visiting them frequently.

One day she was sitting in the park with a cousin of Vadek's. They were confronted by a Russian who demanded to be given some of the bread Ana was eating. When the cousin refused, explaining that Ana was two months pregnant and desperately needed food, the Russian shot him dead. Next to her. On the park bench.

It was a truly terrible time to be in Poland. No-one was safe and everyone lived in fear.

Vadek and Ana did meet again – twenty-seven years later, when he returned. It was an emotional and difficult meeting for both of them. So much had been lost, cruelly taken away, and could never be replaced. It was impossible to turn back the clock. However, they continued to keep in touch, and saw each other whenever Vadek was in Poland, remaining close friends until the day he died.

Stanislaw, Vadek's youngest brother, who had been just a few months old when they were parted, was now able to meet the brother he did not know. He died of cancer in 1985.

Roman married Henja, whose brother had been shot by the Germans. Roman died in 2012 on the farm in Kapice, where Henja still lives with their son, Tadek, who now runs the farm with his son Pawel; the farm will one day be passed on to his grandson, Konrad.

Basyl stayed in England and did indeed stand up as Vadek's best man when he married Irene, then became godfather to my sister Lynn and to me. Basyl never returned to Poland, as every member of his family had been killed during the war; he married and had a family in Nottingham, never losing touch with Vadek.

Jerzy had been sent to Auschwitz. He survived, though he never fully recovered from his ordeal. He and Vadek met again many years later in Bialystok.

Konrad, Vadek's Warsaw University friend and a resistance fighter, had lost his hearing as a result of torture, but he survived and relocated to England. Vadek continued to meet him at the Polish Club in London, until he died in the late 1990s.

For **every Polish veteran**, the ban on their attendance at the Victory Parade in 1945 was the final betrayal. It took sixty years for the UK to make amends; on 10 July 2005 it was the Polish standards that formed the vanguard of the sixtieth anniversary march along the Mall. That form of reparation, however, came too late for most of those who had fought so bravely for freedom.

General Tadeusz Bór-Komorowski survived Colditz and spent the rest of his life in London, dying peacefully in 1971.,

Major-General Władysław Anders, the leader of the Second Polish Army Corps, was able to make a return visit to Poland and also lived out the rest of his life in England, where he died on 12 May 1970.

In **Poland** over the decades, state police had enforced Communist Party rule with the threat of violent retribution and imprisonment – yet despite this, opposition continued with illegal protests, for the Polish people never accepted Soviet interference in the running of their country or the presence of the Red Army in the streets. The protests reached a peak in the late 1970s and early 1980s, when food shortages and high prices fuelled public protests, and the eyes of the world began to take notice. A shipyard worker in Gdansk (formerly Danzig) named Lech Wałęsa, despite constant surveillance and imprisonment, encouraged protests and reform.

So Solidarity, the first independent trade union in the Soviet bloc, was born. Though he was imprisoned and Solidarity banned in 1982, the surge for freedom had taken hold and could no longer be contained..

It was in 1989 with the rise of the Solidarity movement that books could at long last be published in Poland about the Polish army and the Battle of Monte Cassino. The pressure from the people of Poland turned the tide against Communist control, and an agreement was signed in 1989 to hold new elections with less Russian influence. That same year, Soviet authorities finally admitted to the existence of the Secret Protocol, the wartime agreement that had partitioned Poland and other territories. Wałęsa was freed, and in 1990 he became the new Polish president. At last the walls of Communism were tumbling down, and nothing in the Eastern bloc would be the same again.

And after many years of denial, the Russian president, Mikhail Gorbachev, publicly admitted Russian responsibility for the massacre of the Polish officers at Katyń – but Gorbachev fell short of making a full apology. Historian Gerhard Weinberg established that Stalin had wanted to deprive a potential future Polish military of a large portion of its talent, in order to reduce the likelihood of any attempt to rise against him. Stalin had signed the death order on 5 March 1940, after an urgent memorandum from the head of the NKVD, Lavrentiy Beria, stating: 'all these hardened and uncompromising enemies of the Soviet Authority must be declared guilty and executed'. In 1953 – thirteen years to the day of signing the order – Stalin died, of a massive heart attack, on 5 March.

Wojtek the bear came from Iran to Britain with the soldiers he had fought alongside, and lived out his days in Edinburgh Zoo. He died in 1963 aged twenty-three.

Most of the former Polish soldiers gradually adapted and accepted their new life in England and other countries they now called home – but they never forgot the oath they had made in Italy, that last summer of 1946 at the Polish War Cemetery for the Fallen at Monte Cassino: 'One with the desire of the Nation, in Poland and in exile, we solemnly swear to carry on the fight for the freedom of our country, no matter in what conditions it befalls us to live and work.'

The achievements of the Polish Army Corps during the war, and the role of the Polish 303 Squadron in the Battle of Britain have been neglected by many historians; this is due in part to the restrictions imposed by the Communist regime, which refused to allow any recognition of the Poles' involvement in the war. Unbiased information was non-existent, and even after the fall of Communism, the Russians were, unsurprisingly, reluctant to yield such little information as remained. Now, with the passing of time, interest has waned. As for what happened to the Polish soldiers in the Russian labour camps, there are only the accounts from the few survivors to tell the tale.

Dedicated to the gallant Polish soldiers who fought and fell at Monte Cassino is a song composed by Feliks Konarski on the battlefield:

Excerpt from 'Red Poppies on Monte Cassino/ *Czerwone Maki na Monte Cassino*'

Red poppies on Monte Cassino, instead of dew drank Polish blood,
As the soldiers crushed them in falling, for their
anger was more potent than death.
Years will pass and ages will roll, but traces of bygone days will stay
And the poppies on Monte Cassino will be all the
redder for having quaffed Polish blood.
The soldiers charged through fire like madmen, countless were hit and
fell, like the cavalry at Somosierra, like the men at Rokitno years ago.

They attacked with fire and with fury, and they won their objective.

They reached the summit, and their white and scarlet standard they placed on the ruins 'midst clouds.